RIVERS
of the
WORLD

The Ganges

Titles in the Rivers of the World series include:

The Amazon
The Ganges
The Mississippi
The Nile
The Rhine

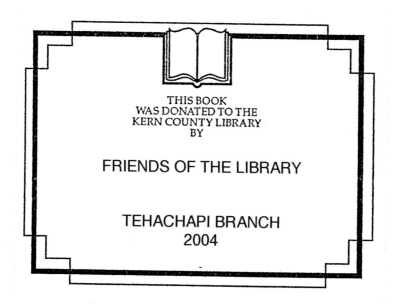

RIVERS
~of the~
WORLD

The Ganges

James Barter

LUCENT
BOOKS ®

THOMSON

★
™

GALE

San Diego • Detroit • New York • San Francisco • Cleveland • New Haven, Conn. • Waterville, Maine • London • Munich

On Cover: An Indian boatman plies the edge of the Ganges.

© 2003 by Lucent Books. Lucent Books is an imprint of The Gale Group, Inc.,
a division of Thomson Learning, Inc.

Lucent Books® and Thomson Learning™ are trademarks used herein under license.

For more information, contact
Lucent Books
27500 Drake Rd.
Farmington Hills, MI 48331-3535
Or you can visit our Internet site at http://www.gale.com

LIBRARY OF CONGRESS CATALOGING-IN-PUBLICATION DATA

Barter, James, 1946–
   The Ganges / by James E. Barter
p. cm. — (Rivers of the world series)
Summary: Discusses the source, course, and tributaries of the Ganges River, its spiritual
significance, its use for agriculture and industry, and its problems with pollution.
Includes bibliographical references and index.
   ISBN 1-59018-060-7 (hardback : alk. paper)
   1. Ganges River (India and Bangladesh)—Juvenile literature. 2. Ganges River Valley
(India and Bangladesh)—Juvenile literature. [1. Ganges River (India and Bangladesh)]
I. Title. II. Rivers of the world (Lucent Books)
   DS485 .G25 B37 2003
   954'.1—dc21
                                           2002005163

Printed in the United States of America

Contents

● ● ● ● ● ● ● ● ● ● ● ● ●

Foreword
••••••••••••

Human history and rivers are inextricably intertwined. Of all the geologic wonders of nature, none has played a more central and continuous role in the history of civilization than rivers. Fanning out across every major landmass except the Antarctic, all great rivers wove an arterial network that played a pivotal role in the inception of early civilizations and in the evolution of today's modern nation-states.

More than ten thousand years ago, when nomadic tribes first began to settle into small, stable communities, they discovered the benefits of cultivating crops and domesticating animals. These incipient civilizations developed a dependence on continuous flows of water to nourish and sustain their communities and food supplies. As small agrarian towns began to dot the Asian and African continents, the importance of rivers escalated as sources of community drinking water, as places for washing clothes, for sewage removal, for food, and as means of transportation. One by one, great riparian civilizations evolved whose collective fame is revered today, including ancient Mesopotamia, between the Tigris and Euphrates Rivers; Egypt, along the Nile; India, along the Ganges and Indus Rivers; and China, along the Yangtze. Later, for the same reasons, early civilizations in the Americas gravitated to the major rivers of the New World such as the Amazon, Mississippi, and Colorado.

For thousands of years, these rivers admirably fulfilled their role in nature's cycle of birth, death, and renewal. The waters also supported the rise of nations and their expanding populations. As hundreds and then thousands of cities sprang up along major rivers, today's modern nations emerged and discovered modern uses for the rivers. With more mouths to feed than ever before, great irrigation canals supplied by river water fanned out across the landscape, transforming parched land into mile upon mile of fertile cropland. Engineers developed the mathematics needed to throw great concrete dams across rivers to control occasional flooding and to store trillions of gallons of water to irrigate crops during the hot summer months. When the great age of electricity arrived, engineers added to the demands placed on rivers by using their cascading water to drive huge hydroelectric turbines to light and heat homes and skyscrapers in urban settings. Rivers also played a major role in the development of modern factories as sources of water for processing a variety of commercial goods and as a convenient place to discharge various types of refuse.

For a time, civilizations and rivers functioned in harmony. Such a benign relationship, however, was not destined to last. At the end of the twentieth century, scientists confirmed the opinions of environmentalists: The viability of all major rivers of the world was threatened. Urban populations could no longer drink the fetid water, masses of fish were dying from chemical toxins, and microorganisms critical to the food chain were disappearing along with the fish species at the top of the chain. The great hydroelectric dams had altered the natural flow of rivers blocking migratory fish routes. As the twenty-first century unfolds, all who have contributed to spoiling the rivers are now in agreement that immediate steps must be taken to heal the rivers if their partnership with civilization is to continue.

Each volume in the Lucent Rivers of the World Series tells the unique and fascinating story of a great river and its people. The significance of rivers to civilizations is emphasized to highlight both their historical role and the present situation. Each volume illustrates the idiosyncrasies of one great river in terms of its physical attributes, the plants and animals that depend on it, its role in ancient and modern cultures, how it served the needs of the people, the misuse of the river, and steps now being taken to remedy its problems.

Introduction

Troubled Sacred Water

The water of the Ganges is sacred to Hindus. It has been worshiped for thirty-five hundred years as water of the goddess *Ganga*, who delivered it to Earth from the skies. So central is the Ganges to Hindu identity that even the word *Hindu* is a derivation of the Sanskrit word *sindhu*, meaning "river." Hindu scripture celebrates the spiritual link between people and rivers, and of all rivers of the world, the Ganges occupies the highest level of esteem. According to Hindu tradition, by bathing in the Ganges, one can wash away all sins and begin anew, cleansed from the imperfections of the past. The purity of its waters is also said to heal the body, grant wishes, bestow salvation, and guarantee eternal life for the spirit.

Bathing in the waters of the Ganges is a Hindu ritual and obligation. Many of the faithful adherents bathe daily in its waters and celebrate Hindu holidays that commemorate the significance of the river in their lives. Those living far from the banks of the Ganges save containers of Ganges water for sacred moments requiring the anointing by holy water. No river in the world plays a more significant religious role—from birth to death—in the lives of its people than *Ma Ganga* ("Mother Ganges").

The Ganges is also the center of the economic, social, and cultural lives of the hundreds of millions of people living along its banks. Emerging from the central Himalayas, the river flows through the north Indian plains providing for the needs of 40 percent of the nation's people before it empties into the Bay of Bengal. As the center of life for the nation's teeming population, the everyday demands placed on the river seem endless. It is called upon to irrigate crops, provide fish to eat, quench thirsts, provide transportation, generate electricity, drain away human and industrial sewage, and act as a watery burial ground. It is a meeting point for both the rich and poor, all of whose lives depend upon the continuous flow of its waters. Jawaharlal Nehru, the first prime minister of India, in 1950 commented on the significance of the Ganges:

People gather on the banks of the Ganges River, the center of life for the millions of people who depend on its waters for survival.

> The Ganga, especially, is the river of India, beloved of her people, round which are intertwined her memories, her hopes and fears, her songs of triumph, her victories and her defeats. She has been a symbol of India's age-long culture and civilization, ever changing, ever flowing, and yet ever the same Ganga.[1]

Unfortunately for the Ganges, the love and reverence that Indians feel for its mystical waters threaten its future. Hindu scripture teaches that the river's waters are pure, and for thousands of years Hindus accepted this literal view in spite of mounting evidence that its pollution levels are among the highest in the world. Until recently, attempts to reduce pollution and to clean the river have been rejected by the Hindu faithful who believed that the holy waters of the river were self-cleansing.

Within the past thirty years, foul-smelling odors and masses of floating dead fish have told a story even devout Hindus can no longer ignore. Environmental studies have uncovered excessive levels of toxic industrial effluents and municipal sewage that are debilitating the sacred life-giving waters of the river. In 1985, in response to a call for action, the Indian government initiated the Ganges Action Plan (GAP) aimed at cleaning the river and imposing restrictions on the use of the river to dispose of industrial and municipal wastes.

The fanfare and optimism that greeted GAP in 1985 faded by 2000. Poorly conceived solutions, inability to provide electricity for water pumps, underestimation of the ravages of highly toxic chemicals, and collusion between factory owners and corrupt politicians have undermined the plan's objectives. According to several independent studies, the water quality of the Ganges is worse today than it was in 1985.

At this time, no new proposals have been put forth for saving one of the world's great rivers. What compounds the problem is that the population of the Ganges Basin is increasing at an alarming rate. Demographers, biologists, and environmentalists agree that this magnificent river will not be able to bear the increasing pressure that an estimated 1 billion people will place on it by 2050. Of all the world's rivers, perhaps none faces as bleak a future as does the Ganges.

1
· · · · · · · · · ·
The River from Ice

The Ganges is the largest river system on the Indian subcontinent. Rising out of the Himalayas near India's border with Tibet, the river gradually swells and wends its way south before abruptly turning east as it strikes across the flat northern plains of India. When the river is within two hundred miles of the Bay of Bengal, it crosses the Bangladesh border where its name changes to the Padma. From there it spills into the bay, staining it a muddy hue for more than three hundred miles out to sea. A satellite photograph mapping this 1,560-mile-long journey reveals a flourishing basin covering 416,000 square miles, which is home to an estimated 400 million of India's 1 billion people and another 25 million in Bangladesh.

The Ganges' surge is unique among major rivers because of its mix of frigid and tepid water. Geology and climate account for its fountainhead of cascading water from melting Himalayan snows and glaciers. Added to these icy waters are hot torrential rains dropped during the summer monsoons—waters that regularly reach temperatures between 110° and 120° Fahrenheit. As this unusual mix of extreme temperatures moves down the

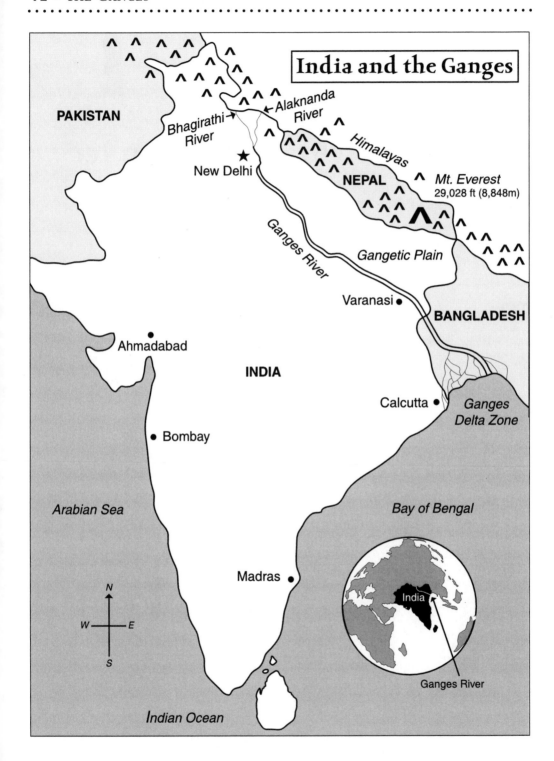

India and the Ganges

PAKISTAN

Bhagirathi River

Alaknanda River

★ New Delhi

Himalayas

NEPAL

Mt. Everest
29,028 ft (8,848m)

Ganges River

Gangetic Plain

Varanasi ●

BANGLADESH

Ahmadabad ●

INDIA

Calcutta ●

Ganges Delta Zone

● Bombay

Arabian Sea

Bay of Bengal

Madras ●

N

W — E

S

India

Indian Ocean

Ganges River

mountains and eastward across northern India, a network of hundreds of tributaries joins the procession to the sea. When this torrent reaches the river's mouth, it blasts 30 million gallons of water per second into the bay.

The Himalayan Zone

Scientists divide the Ganges' fifteen-hundred-mile length into three distinct geologic and climatic zones: the Himalayan, the Gangetic Plain, and the Delta. The Himalayan zone, which is located along the slopes of the Himalayan mountain range near the Tibetan border, is the shortest and most spectacular of the three zones. In this 155-mile stretch, the river rises at its source among the commanding jagged snowcapped mountains and cascades through deep gorges and over a sequence of icy waterfalls until it settles onto the Gangetic Plain at the city of Hardwar (also called Haridwar).

Limnologists, as scientists who study bodies of fresh water such as rivers and lakes are known, recognize two headstreams of the Ganges: the Bhagirathi and Alaknanda Rivers. The Bhagirathi is the farthest from the Bay of Bengal and is therefore considered to be the Ganges' true source, but the Alaknanda is also credited as being one of the headstreams because it begins at a higher altitude of 25,600 feet, not far from the Bhagirathi, and because the two join downstream at the city of Devprayag.

The Bhagirathi begins its long trek to the sea as a stream of pure sparkling glacial water issuing forth from a cave at the south end of the Great Gangotri Glacier, a five-by-twenty-five-mile tongue of ice. This cave, located near the village of Gaumukh at an elevation of thirteen thousand feet, is considered by Hindus to be the meeting place of heaven and earth. To those who come here to dip into its bitterly cold waters, this place is sacred.

Many other Himalayan glaciers are ever-renewing sources of water for the Ganges as well. In summer and autumn, millions of cubic feet of ice melt each second, sustaining the Ganges and its tributaries. Scientists are not certain of the precise volume released each year due to the unpredictability of temperatures and to their inability to access and measure many small streams. An understanding of the huge quantities of water stored within the glacial ice, however, can be grasped by the fact that the Gangotri Glacier alone has a constant volume of roughly

Melting Glaciers

Geologists explain that the Himalayan glaciers are constantly adding and losing mass at roughly the same rate. They also point out that the melting process owes as much to pressure as it does to the sun's warmth. The pressure exerted by millions of tons of ice generates substantial heat on the bottom layers of ice. These temperatures are further increased by friction as the glaciers slowly crawl forward at the rate of between five and ten feet a year. The reason glaciers do not always advance down valleys is because their leading edges usually break off and melt. Geologists who have analyzed the melting ice at the Gangotri Glacier have been able to determine it to be about four hundred years old.

For the past eons, glacial fluctuations and change have gone largely unnoticed because the annual melt has always provided enough water to swell the Ganges and its tributaries.

Recently, however, geologists studying the status of major Himalayan glaciers have noted that many appear to be retreating at an alarmingly fast rate. If this retreat does not reverse or slow, scientists fear that the water supply for the 400 million Indians living in the Ganges Basin could be in peril.

Geologists studying glacial formations during the 1990s had expected the many glaciers feeding the Ganges to grow in mass as the result of several severe winters. Instead, many are shrinking at the rate of fifty feet a year, much faster than ever recorded in the past. In an interview published in *Science* magazine on August 28, 1998, geologist Joseph T. Gergan of the Wadia Institute of Himalayan Geology said, "It has been a phenomenal melt rate this year."

One major ice source for the Ganges, the twenty-five-mile-long Gangotri Glacier, has also been six cubic miles, which is equivalent to nearly 7 trillion gallons of water.

As the Bhagirathi departs the cave, it plunges headlong into a series of cascades as the river drops into the deep and spectacular Bhaironghati gorge. Of all the major gorges on the Ganges, this one is considered to be the most beautiful because of its deep glens and forests of cedar,

retreating, although the precise rate is unknown because there is no permanent monitoring station there. Professor Gergan and others believe the unexpected melt is a sign of global warming. The unusually rapid retreats of many glaciers provide evidence that the past five years may have been the hottest in the past millennium.

Should the glacial retreat continue at its current rate for the next twenty-five years, scientists predict many long-term consequences. Most dramatic will be an unusual swelling of the Ganges that could easily destroy hundreds of cities and towns along the river. Worst of all, the Delta zone could become completely submerged for long periods.

With the source of the river greatly diminished, the long-term outlook for the Ganges is for a greatly reduced flow. If the bulk of each glacier disappears and is not replenished, the Ganges would receive less water and begin to shrink, rendering the entire Ganges Basin barren of vegetation except along the immediate banks.

In recent years Himalayan glaciers (background) have melted at a rate much faster than in previously recorded years.

birch, oak, and pine that border the river. As the river flows through the gorges, it picks up silt, mostly consisting of pulverized rock, that will be deposited downstream. At this point on its trek to the Bay of Bengal, the river is still narrow and shallow enough to be crossed on horseback.

From its glacial sources, the Bhagirathi cascades to the city of Devprayag, where it joins the Alaknanda and first takes the name Ganges or *Ganga* in Hindi. The second century B.C. Indian poet Kalidasa composed a poem called *The Cloud Messenger* in which he describes the water's descent,

> Fly then where Ganga on the king of mountains
> Falls like a flight of stairs from heaven let down
> For the sons of men; she hurls her billowy fountains
> Like hands to grasp the moon on Shiva's crown
> And laughs her foamy laugh at Gauri's [Shiva's wife]
> jealous crown.[2]

From here, the river continues its dramatic descent to the city of Hardwar (which means "God's door") at the base of the Himalayas where the Gangetic Plain zone begins at an elevation of one thousand feet. At this point, in its journey 155 miles from the Gangotri Glacier, the river has dropped at the ratio of 1:68, meaning that for every sixty-eight feet of horizontal run the river's elevation dropped one foot. This gradient is so acute that river travel by boat upstream from Hardwar is impossible.

Limnologists point out that an extremely steep gradient that can span such a long distance is a rare occurrence among rivers. Precipitous individual cascades are common on most rivers, but they are generally isolated or of short duration, unlike the chaining sequences of waterfalls cascading down the Himalayas.

The Gangetic Plain Zone

In the twelve-hundred-mile-long Gangetic Plain zone—the longest of the three zones—the river slowly meanders south and then abruptly veers east across northern India until it reaches the Farakka Dam, which is twelve miles from India's border with Bangladesh. Lying south of and parallel to the Himalayas, the Ganges Basin, including all of the river's tributaries, extends over an area of about 270,000 square miles, varying in width from less than a mile to over 150 miles. The Ganges departs Hardwar at an elevation of one thousand feet and arrives at the dam at an elevation of two hundred feet, meaning that in many places, the drop in elevation is imperceptible and the current is so slow that it is difficult to tell in which direction the river is flowing.

The river current is slow, but as the Ganges threads its way east through the Gangetic Plain, its volume of water increases as several major tributaries join its journey to the sea. Three of the major tributaries rise high in the Himalaya Mountains, just as the Ganges does. The first tributary to join the Ganges is the Yamuna River, which begins at the Yamuna Glacier at an elevation of 20,500 feet. The Yamuna runs parallel to the Ganges from Tibet for 850 miles until their convergence at the city of Allahabad.

Two hundred and twenty-five miles east of Allahabad is the city Patna where the Ganges is joined by three more major rivers: the Gandak, Ghaghara, and the Sone. The Gandak and Ghaghara both have their sources in the Himalaya Mountains. As these rivers flow south out of the mountains, each turns east to eventually join the Ganges, bringing along rich deposits of silt. The Sone is the sole major tributary that flows north before joining the other tributaries at Patna.

The Gangetic Plain, watered by the Ganges and its many tributaries, is the site of most of the Ganges Basin's crop production. This plain is famed as the world's most extensive tract of highly fertile soil, thanks to the silt that is deposited here during periods in which the river overflows its banks. Bore samples have disclosed a remarkable silt depth of six thousand feet. Because of this thick layer of silt, crops here are among the most bountiful in the world.

The Delta Zone

The two-hundred-mile-long Delta zone, from the Farakka Dam to the Bay of Bengal, accounts for the remainder of the Ganges' course. Just downriver from the dam, as the Ganges approaches sea level, it departs from its narrowly defined riverbed and fans out, forming a two-hundred-mile-wide arc of land that is saturated by thousands of small rivers and streams. Geologists explain that this Delta phenomenon is the result of annual deposits of billions of tons of silt carried down the river. Over hundreds of thousands of years, the Delta has slowly but steadily grown, displacing the ocean's water in the process. Geologists estimate that the Ganges Delta covers a forty-thousand-square-mile area, making it the world's largest river delta.

When the Ganges arrives at the Delta, its impact is magnified by its joining with one of its major tributaries,

A satellite photo shows the Ganges Delta Zone, where the river begins to fan out before meeting the Bay of Bengal (right).

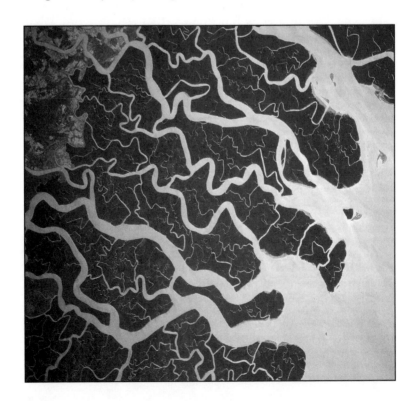

the Brahmaputra River. The Brahmaputra begins its eighteen-hundred-mile-long journey from western Tibet, flowing east along the northern slopes of the Himalayas for one thousand miles before abruptly turning south at the eastern end of the mountain kingdom of Bhutan. At that point it cuts through a pass in the Himalayas and joins the Ganges within one hundred miles of the Bay of Bengal. At the Delta, as the two rivers approach each other, they spread out across the bay, where the average elevation above sea level never exceeds a mere nine feet.

At such a low elevation, the Delta zone is subject to flooding on a regular basis. During the heavy rains of the monsoon season, when billions of gallons of river water gush across the Delta each hour, the entire area is swamped. This situation is further worsened during periods of extreme tidal activity, because high ocean tides can reach twenty feet above the normal low tide. When the tides are high and the Ganges is flooding, the Delta disappears beneath the mix of salt water and freshwater.

The Indian Monsoon

Limnologists studying the Delta recognize that together with the water that originates in the Himalaya Mountains, the monsoon rains play a major role in the life of the Ganges. The Indian monsoon is a climatic phenomenon in which prevailing winds reverse direction on a seasonal basis. Its winds generally blow from the southwest during summer, bringing hot winds and heavy rains to the Ganges Basin, and then blow from the northeast during the winter, bringing drought. Within the three zones, the variation in rainfall between winter and summer is dramatic. In all three zones, the winter drought means that less than one inch of rain falls during the month of December. In August, however, the Himalayan zone receives sixteen to twenty inches, the Gangetic Plain between eight and sixteen inches, and the Delta between sixteen and eighteen inches. When the wet monsoon begins in June, the Ganges is able to accommodate the

Heavy rains from the Indian monsoon can provide up to twenty inches of rain during the wettest months, and serve as a major source of water for the Ganges River.

rainfall without flooding its banks. As the rains continue to arrive in July and hit their peak in August, however, the banks of the Ganges are overwhelmed in many areas.

The predictable flooding is welcomed by farmers for the water that saturates crops along the riverbanks. Crop selection in the floodplains is determined by the amount of flooding expected; light flooding is desirable for cultivation of vegetables and grains such as wheat and barley, while heavy flooding is favorable for growing rice and sugarcane. These floods have been taking place for many millennia, and the inhabitants of the Ganges Basin know how to deal with them. They not only know what crops to plant and where to plant them but also how to build their homes away from the path of the floods, either on mounds of dirt or on bamboo poles.

Geology of the Ganges

The Ganges floods and flows where it does because of geologic activity that shaped the land millions of years ago. The Ganges River Basin is shaped like a large flat funnel

The Himalayas

In Sanskrit *hima* means "snow" and *alaya* means "home." This spectacular arc of snowcapped peaks is the largest mountain range in the world. The Himalayas are also the source for dozens of rivers that flow down the north and south slopes. The Himalayas stretch 1,600 miles from the 26,658-foot tall Nanga Parbat in Pakistan to the 25,445-foot Namcha Barwa peak in Tibet. The width of the Himalayas ranges from 155 to 220 miles and their total area is roughly 300,000 square miles.

The Himalayas are the source of dozens of rivers which eventually join the Ganges.

The Himalayas are divided into three longitudinal belts: the greater, the lesser, and the outer Himalayas. The greater Himalayas are those mountains most well known to the public. These are the peaks that most often attract professional mountaineers. The heights of the peaks are generally above 16,000 feet with 110 of them above 25,000. The tallest, Mt. Everest, stands 29,028 feet and was first climbed by Edmund Hillary and Tenzing Norgay in 1953.

The height of the Himalayas guarantees annual average temperatures well below freezing. Because of such low temperatures, this is one of the most abundant areas for snow and ice which, in spite of the low temper-atures, melts at the rate of billions of cubic feet of water annually. This enormous melt provides the west and east slopes with white-water rapids that cascade down to the plains below, providing the nations of India, China, Nepal, and Pakistan with much of their water supply.

Geologists estimate that this mountain range is relatively young at 25 million years old. They also explain that because of the continued movement of the earth's tectonic plates, the Himalayas continue to rise at the rate of two and a half inches a year.

that captures water from melted snow and ice cascading down the southern slopes of the Himalayan mountain range and directs it across northern India and into the Bay of Bengal. This funnel shape was formed several million years ago when the Himalayas were created as a result of the movement of large continental landmasses in a slow process called continental drift.

The immense Himalayas began to form between 40 million and 50 million years ago when the drifting Indian and Eurasian landmasses collided. The pressure caused the land to be thrust skyward—called an upwarp by geologists—thereby forming the jagged Himalayan peaks. South of the great upheaval at the base of the Himalayas, the Gangetic Plain was formed. The plain was originally under salt water, but the silt brought from the mountains by the rivers gradually displaced the seawater.

As the Ganges and its major tributaries continue depositing enormous amounts of silt from the majestic Himalayas, the river basin will continue to expand eastward. Geologists speculate that over the next million years, if this cycle of erosion in the Himalayas and deposit of silt in the Bay of Bengal continues, the Bay of Bengal will gradually disappear. Unless humans somehow intervene, this process will form the most fertile land in the world as the Himalayan mountain range gradually erodes.

Amazing Animals Along the Ganges

Thanks to the dramatic drop in elevation over the river's course to the sea, the Ganges River Basin is home for a far greater variety of fascinating animals than most rivers of comparable length. Each of the three zones forms a unique habitat that provides for a stunning variety of animals, many of which are not found anywhere else. All of the animals living along the Ganges are divided into two general categories, however: those that dwell in the river and those that come to drink and hunt.

The Himalayan zone, covered by snow and ice most of the year, is the perfect habitat for several wild mammals.

The brown bear, red panda, and snow leopard are occa-sionally seen at the river. The brown bear thrives primarily on soft leafy plants and berries but will occasionally eat fish and rodents. Although rarely seen, this bear is not endan-gered. The red panda, however, is endangered. This animal, which resembles a large raccoon, is exclusively an herbi-vore, feeding on huge quantities of leaves. Because leaves provide so little nourishment, red pandas must eat contin-uously during their waking hours to sustain themselves.

Of the three, the snow leopard is considered to be the most beautiful, the most exotic, and the most endangered. During summer, these cats roam at a height of twelve thousand to twenty-five thousand feet but in winter they come down as low as six thousand feet. The adult snow leopard is four feet long and its fur, a grayish white color with black rosettes, blends well in the snow and rocks. The cat's most notable characteristic is its extraordinarily long tail, about three and a half feet, nearly as long as its body. The snow leopard typically hunts along rivers for smaller mammals but is not reluctant to enter streams to catch fish.

The Gangetic zone is home to 140 species of fish, 67 species of birds, and an impressive array of land animals, including the Asian ele-phant, the rhesus monkey, and the golden jackal. However, of all the river ani-mals in this zone, none is better adapted to the water than the Indian gharial, a species of crocodile.

The gharial has an extremely slender snout that it uses for catching fish in fast-moving waters. Although gharials can grow up to twenty feet in length, they pose no danger to

An Indian gharial uses its sharp teeth and long snout for catching fish in the Ganges' fast-moving waters.

humans. Considered timid animals, gharials are content to feed on small fish and turtles. Although it occasionally leaves the water to bask in the sun or to nest, its legs are not strong enough to raise its body off the ground to stalk and hunt land animals.

The Delta zone, which is subject to frequent flooding, is home to a variety of aquatic and semiaquatic animals. Deer, fish, monkeys, and even rhinoceroses sometimes roam this vast delta. This zone is also home to the most revered, admired, and feared animal of the Ganges Basin—the Bengal tiger, the largest of the big cats. The Bengal tiger is a carnivore, and an adult, which may be ten feet long and weigh seven hundred pounds can and will run down horses and cattle and dive in the water to catch large fish and porpoises. As a species, Bengal tigers even snare unsuspecting humans at the rate of thirty a year.

The Bengal tiger is India's official animal, but it is endangered. Its beautiful orange, black, and white coat, which serves as effective camouflage, also places it in great

A Bengal tiger pounces into a stream in pursuit of its next meal.

danger because poachers kill the animal for its skin. This animal is also killed for its body parts, which are used in some Asian cultures as medicines and aphrodisiacs.

Ganges' Plants

More than the diversity of animal life, the Ganges is notable for the variety of plants along its course. Botanists estimate that there are about forty-five thousand species

The Ganges River Dolphin

The Ganges River dolphin is one of the most unusual animals in the river. The estimated current population is a mere five thousand, placing it on the endangered species list. This mammal inhabits the Ganges, Brahmaputra, and Meghna Rivers of India, Bangladesh, Nepal, and Bhutan.

The Ganges River dolphin is easily identifiable by its long snout, which thickens toward the tip revealing large teeth caused by a mouth-line that curves upward. The eight-foot, two-hundred-pound body is stocky with a rounded belly, the flippers are large and paddle-shaped, and there is a low triangular hump in place of a true dorsal fin. The forehead is steep and the blowhole is on the left of the head, above the tiny eye. This dolphin is gray-brown in color with a distinctive pinkish belly.

Ganges River dolphins travel either as couples or as individuals.

The dolphins are effectively blind— all they can do is detect the direction and intensity of light. This blindness is one of the reasons why these dolphins swim on one side underwater, with one flipper trailing in the muddy riverbed. The physical touch gives the dolphins important information about their surroundings and helps them to find food. Without effective eyes, they navigate entirely by a sophisticated echolocation system that is similar to sonar.

The large human population along the Ganges is primarily responsible for the endangered status of the dolphin. Most dangerous to the dolphin are the dams, boat traffic, chemical pollution, being trapped in fishing gear, and illegal poaching. Many dolphins are taken deliberately by tribal peoples who annually catch thirty to forty for their oil and meat or to use as fishing bait.

of plant life in India. Of these, half can be found in the Ganges Basin. Aside from the value of plants as food, traditional Indian doctors use twenty-five hundred types of plants to create various medicines. In addition, modern medicine finds use for the plants that grow here. Quinine, digitalis, and morphine, which are commonly used around the world, all come from plants that grow somewhere in the Ganges Basin.

Of the three zones, the one with the sparsest vegetation is the Himalayan, due to the cold and thin atmosphere caused by the high altitude. In spite of the harsh climate and geology, however, stands of many forest species such as pine, spruce, fir, oak, poplar, walnut, and birch thrive. At lower Himalayan altitudes below the snow line, vegetation includes shrubs growing close to the river as well as a few wild flowers that can survive the snows such as blue poppies, edelweiss, and rhododendrons. Various mosses and lichens also thrive at these lower elevations.

As the river flows across the lower and warmer elevations of the Gangetic Plain, the variety of vegetation increases dramatically. Botanists estimate that 16 percent of the basin area is forest and 9.9 percent is a mixture of crops and natural vegetation. The most-valued and revered species of vegetation is the banyan tree, India's national plant. This large tree has wide-spreading leafy branches that extend one hundred feet in diameter. The banyan is easily recognized by its numerous aerial roots growing down from the branches, which take root in the soil and help to support the tree's tremendous weight. By using the prop roots, the banyan can continue to spread. Besides the tree's distinctive appearance, it also serves as a gathering place for people and animals. The tree functions as a nesting area for many birds, a home for monkeys, and a community center for villagers who use the shade as a place for relaxation, conversation, and an impromptu market for selling produce and craft items.

Of the three zones, however, vegetation in the watery Delta exceeds the combined variety in the other two zones. Of the thousands of species, the most plentiful and valuable is the mangrove tree. Thriving in the swampy brackish waters of the Delta, mangroves produce tangled masses of arching roots that are exposed during low tides. The trees are harvested for lumber, and a variety of resins can be extracted from the wood and used for many industrial applications. These trees are also home to monkeys, fish, and crocodiles that breed and feed in the safety of the underwater root systems, and hundreds of extraordinarily beautiful birds that nest in the branches.

With such a variety of useful and beautiful plants and animals living in or near the river, it is small wonder that humans came to revere it for its significance in their lives. Because it was their source of water, food, and transportation, residents along the banks of the Ganges early on developed a spiritual appreciation for its mystical waters.

2

·········

The Waters of Creation

Great rivers have always been the focal point of early civilizations. The Ganges, like the Nile in Egypt, the Yangtze in China, and the Tigris and Euphrates in ancient Mesopotamia, were all centers of great cultures. The earliest peoples to occupy the Ganges Basin did so for the same reasons as their earlier counterparts in Mesopotamia and Egypt—the river brought life where it flowed, irrigating crops, providing fish, transporting goods, and protecting against foreign invaders. The life-giving attributes of the Ganges, therefore, were not unique, but were nonetheless critical to defining the culture that grew along its banks.

Agriculture

Of all the river's functions, none was more crucial than its role in producing food. Crop production for early settlers along the banks of the Ganges depended on the monsoon. Lacking even primitive forms of irrigation, farmers saw crop production suffer during abnormal monsoon conditions. An overly active monsoon caused severe flooding that caused crops to rot in the fields, while too mild a monsoon brought drought conditions that left crops to wither in the parched hard soil.

The intensity of the monsoon, however, was not the only climatic variable. The timing of the monsoon's arrival was the other factor that determined the success of the annual harvest. Crops suffered from either a late or early start to the rainy season. Crops also suffered in the midst of the monsoon if an extended break in the rains occurred. No less serious was a premature conclusion to the monsoons, which caused otherwise healthy crops to wither before they could mature.

Water and nutrients carried down from the Himalayas make the Gangetic Plain (shown here) ideal for agriculture.

Fortunately for farmers, the monsoons were for the most part consistent. Farmers learned what crops could thrive with normal rainfall, which varied according to specific locations along the Ganges. Areas that received the most flooding were planted with crops such as rice, sugarcane and cotton, which thrived in saturated fields during hot weather. Areas farther from the river that received less floodwater were ideal for grain crops such as wheat, barley, and oats, along with a variety of vegetables.

According to University of Pennsylvania archaeologist Steven Weber, ancient farmers planted a variety of hardy crops that required only minimal water and cultivation. Weber recently unearthed ten thousand ancient seeds from a Ganges excavation site. Crops the farmers grew included several indigenous species of grains, peas, and beans.

In addition to bringing water to croplands, the Ganges also brought a variety of crop-enriching nutrients. Water cascading down the Himalayas carried silt consisting of minerals and organic matter that would then settle out when the river spilled over its banks. During the annual flood season, the floodwaters laid down layers of silt several feet thick. Once the floodwaters receded, farmers planted seeds in the nutritious silt confident that the harvest would be abundant.

Whatever crops were planted, farming techniques were primitive and only the most rudimentary tools were available. Fields were plowed using oxen or, if a farmer were poor, the plow was pulled by his sons and daughters. Using such basic technology, the average farmer could cultivate no more than three to ten acres.

Fishing

Although crop production sustained early dwellers along the Ganges, grain crops could not provide protein needed for a balanced diet. Cattle were plentiful in ancient India, but they were considered sacred by Hindus, and therefore could not be eaten. Fortunately, fish were plentiful in two of the three Ganges zones, the Gangetic Plain and the

Delta. As a result, fish comprised the principal source of protein for early inhabitants of the Ganges Basin.

Each zone provided a different habitat, so the species available to people varied. The Delta was unique because of the regular inundations of salt water from the rising and falling tides. During exceptionally high tides when the westerly winds were strong, ocean waves called tidal bores would sweep several hundred miles inland, sending ten-foot-high waves breaking over the river's banks. The salt water mixed with the freshwater from upriver; certain species of freshwater fish such as carp and catfish thrived in these brackish waters as did saltwater fish swept inland by the tidal bores, such as yellow fin, skipjack, and small tuna. Crustaceans such as shrimp, prawns, and crab would also inhabit the waters of the Delta.

Within the twelve-hundred-mile-long Gangetic zone, the diversity of fish was much richer than in the Delta. Several species of carp were caught including the katla, which grows to six feet and weighs one hundred pounds, and the rohu, which is bluish or brownish in color and three feet long. Besides these fish, freshwater sharks and eels were also plentiful.

Fishermen pursued their quarry using techniques that would change little. Archaeologists have found evidence of ancient metal fishhooks, and ancient murals discovered in modern times depict fishing boats with nets extended out on both sides of the boat. The nets were held in place by long poles at right angles to the boat. As the boats moved through the estuaries of the Delta, the nets were dipped into the water, trapping fish that were then hauled on board.

Fishing along the Gangetic Plain was done either from boats similar to those used in the Delta or by constructing weirs across some of the smaller tributaries. Ancient fish weirs were fencelike structures made of bamboo sticks set close together with only one or two small openings through which fish could pass. Baskets or nets were then placed behind each small opening to trap fish after they passed through the weir.

This painting shows the hunters of ancient India, as described by the Greek historian Herodotus.

Hunting

The waters of the Ganges provided not only a wealth of fish but also a wealth of animals that could be killed for their meat. The Ganges was home to many species of large animals drawn to its waters for survival, such as the crocodile and hippopotamus. Migrating birds could be hunted in large numbers as they landed on the river to search for food and to rest. Many other land animals were drawn to the river's water to quench their thirst and hunters took advantage of this fact and waited nearby in ambush.

The peoples of the Ganges were more fortunate than their counterparts elsewhere in the ancient world in that the game they hunted was larger and therefore capable of feeding more hungry mouths. The fifth-century B.C. Greek historian and traveler Herodotus visited India and reported on the size of wild animals observing, "In India, which, as I observed lately, is the furthest region of the inhabited world towards the east, all the four-footed beasts and the birds are very much bigger than those found elsewhere."[3]

Herodotus went on a hunt and reported that, "The Indians wore cotton dresses, and carried bows of cane, and arrows also of cane with iron at the point."[4]

Four hundred years later, the Greek geographer Strabo also traveled to India and reported the use of hunting dogs that were trained to bring down large game including lions and wild bulls, even though the bulls were sacred to devout Hindus. Upon witnessing a hunt, he commented that the dogs were remarkably tenacious, noting that they "do not let go the object bitten till water is poured down into their nostrils."[5] Strabo reported that these dogs, which he described as being larger than foxes, were capable of holding down an Asiatic lion until hunters arrived to kill their quarry with spears. He also saw a pack of dogs attack and kill a bull that could not escape because one dog had hold of its nose and would not let go regardless of how hard the bull shook.

The largest animals were sometimes stampeded into deep pits where hunters could easily kill them with

Stranger-than-Fiction Hunting Techniques

The first century B.C. *Greek geographer Strabo reported all he saw on his journeys as well as much of what he heard from local peoples. While in India, he reported in his book,* Geography: Book XV: On India, *the following stories told to him about two stranger-than-fiction techniques for hunting apes:*

The capture of the animal [ape] is effected in two ways. It is an imitative animal and takes to flight up in the trees. Now the hunters, when they see an ape seated on a tree, place in sight a bowl containing water and rub their own eyes with it: and then they put down a bowl of bird-lime [a sticky substance] instead of the water, go away, and lie in wait at a distance; and when the animal leaps down and besmears itself with the bird-lime, and when, upon winking, its eyelids are shut together, the hunters approach and take it alive.

Now this is one way, but there is another. They [hunters] put on baggy breeches like trousers and then go away, leaving behind them others that so are shaggy and smeared inside with bird-lime; and when the animals put these on, they are easily captured.

weapons, such as spears and bows and arrows, or keep them alive to perform hard work. No animal was too large for the pits and Strabo reported elephants being captured in pits and later tamed for arduous work in forests and fields. Elephants were also eaten. During a 1997 excavation of a Ganges village, Professor Gregory L. Possehl, of the University of Pennsylvania, reported that: "The villagers apparently were hunters as well as farmers, and they supplemented their diet with wild animals including elephants, a type of wild dog, and a good selection of the local deer and antelope."[6]

Besides hunting with bows and arrows, some peoples of the Ganges practiced falconry. Several cave paintings dating back to 1500 B.C. show a large bird on the fist of a human figure. Grasped in the same fist is a rabbit held by the back legs. Another, somewhat later, painting depicts a small bird of prey perched on the wrist of a man. This painting seems to show jesses, the leather thongs used to secure the bird to the falconer, tied to the bird's feet and passing between the thumb and forefinger of the holder.

Travel on the Ganges

The river's importance for most people living along its banks went far beyond its being the source of their food. The river was also their major transportation route. Although walking was the most common form of travel and cattle-drawn carts were commonly used for transporting goods, boats of various sizes traveled between most of the towns along the Ganges.

Early inhabitants of the Ganges as far back as the fifth and sixth centuries B.C. were able to sail up the river from the Bay of Bengal to the city of Hardwar at the base of the Himalayas. Travel was easy in either direction because the river's current along much of its length was slow enough to ensure smooth sailing. Ancient boats were fitted with sails that could be easily unfurled to take advantage of favorable winds and furled in contrary ones.

The most common early boats plying the river were of wood plank construction using short boards nailed or pegged edge to edge on wood ribs to form the hull. Rarely more than thirty feet long and often shorter, these boats were fitted with a fifteen-foot center mast that carried a single cotton sail. Outfitted in this way, a boat could travel between three and ten miles an hour, depending on the winds and direction of travel. As the boats moved through the water, a tillerman stood at the back of the boat and steered with the wood handle of a rudder extending into the water on one side of the boat. A sixth-century document records the significance of boats to the early inhabitants of northern India in these orders from a priest to: "Take 300 shipwrights [ship builders], go to the upper Ganges, procure timber, build 300 ships, . . . fill them with light wood and come back soon."[7]

The Ganges was the most significant link between the hundreds of towns and cities of northern India. Boats carrying goods and passengers regularly plied the river, keeping people of the Ganges Basin apprised of everyday news as well as of events affecting everyone's life. Towns well away from the river benefited from this transportation link as well. Archaeological excavations at several sites reveal an extensive string of port cities where goods could be stored in regional warehouses for distribution to cities far from the river. Archaeologists excavating these regional distribution centers report finding sophisticated docks for the loading and unloading of freight boats as well as canals that could accommodate smaller barges hauling goods to landlocked settlements.

Early boats not only traveled the river but also plied the Indian Ocean as far south as modern-day Sri Lanka, an island off the southern coast of India, and southeast to the island of Java in the Indonesian archipelago. As trading vessels, these freighters were larger than boats used exclusively on the Ganges, possibly three to four times larger. They would return and unload their cargo at various ports on the Ganges Delta where smaller boats would

Traders use small boats to carry goods from the Ganges Delta to port cities along the Ganges.

carry the goods for the remainder of the trip upriver to major port cities. In this way, much of India was linked to a trading network that extended throughout the ancient world. Early writers record the costs to hire oceangoing boats and make duty payments and tell of silk and pearl trading. During the first centuries B.C. and A.D., when Rome emerged as a dominant Mediterranean civilization, many documents record a brisk spice trade with Rome in exchange for iron tools and farm implements.

As time went on, people built larger boats. By the time Europeans first arrived in India fifteen hundred years later, much larger freighters were reported carrying as much as five hundred tons of salt and other goods. One early European visitor, Peter Mundy, reported that boats on the Ganges contained "several rooms [and were] able to carry a small village with all inhabitants and goods; such was their hugeness."[8]

The Ganges in Hindu Thought

In exchange for all that the Ganges provided for those living along its banks, this great river received spiritual adoration of its users that went far beyond that lavished by peoples along other rivers in the ancient world. Although the ancient Egyptians worshiped the Nile, they did not commit their lives to the river to the same extent as the people of the Ganges Basin did. No other great river was associated with spiritual powers as was the Ganges, known to the ancients as *Ma Ganga*. *Ma Ganga* was venerated as a mother possessing the power to create, pre-

A young prince approaches the deity Ma Ganga (left).

serve, destroy, and then re-create all over again. The physical waters themselves symbolized purification to early Hindus, who believed that drinking or bathing in its waters would lead to *moksha*, or spiritual salvation.

The significance of the Ganges in the lives of its peoples elevated the river to a position of mystical significance. No natural phenomenon was more widely understood, appreciated, beloved, or worshiped than the river was. This giver of life entered all aspects of each Hindu's life. Stories about the creation of the river and the significance of its waters were learned and retold as part of Hindu history and culture. Even birth itself was believed to be a gift of the river, as this ancient Hindu poem from the book of *Katha Upanishad* suggests: "He who was born of old was born of water. Right from the waters, the soul drew forth and shaped a person."[9] This viewpoint is also found in the sacred book *Rig Veda*, which says, "Golden in form is he, like gold to look upon, the Son of the waters."[10] The waters of the Ganges transcended physical characteristics to the realm of the spiritual. They were endowed with powers to protect people's lives, cure diseases, forgive sins, and guarantee new life after death.

The sanctity of the Ganges water meant that it was used by early Hindus for rituals celebrating all rites of passage: birth, marriage, and death as well as the commonplace rituals that greeted the rising and setting of the sun. Water from the river was believed to have a recursive property, meaning any water mixed with even the minutes amount of Ganges water became Ganges water and therefore was capable of healing and other holy properties. In addition, Hindus believed that whatever impurities entered the Ganges' water, it was self-purifying.

A Hindu worshiper meditates at the edge of the Ganges River.

Three Tirthas

Early Hindus attributed miraculous powers to the water of the Ganges. Not only would the water purify one's spirit, it also had the power to heal the body, impart good luck to people's lives, guarantee immortality, and bless

Myth of the Ganges' Origin

As far back as 1500 B.C., the Ganges grew in spiritual importance and many legends were told to explain its origins. The one that has survived and is most popular tells the story of a king named Sagara who had two wives. One wife bore him sixty thousand sons, all of whom were destined to die simultaneously, and the other bore him one son, Asamanjas, who would continue the dynasty.

The sixty thousand sons grew to be great warriors, while the mighty Asamanjas caused so much misery to the populace that his father the king had to expel his own son, although a grandson, Ansuman, was left behind. King Sagara decided to perform a horse ceremony, in which a horse is allowed to roam at will, and is followed by warriors. In this case, the sixty thousand sons were following the horse, but surprisingly, the horse was lost. After much searching, the horse was found in a deep cavern close to where a wise man named Kapila meditated. The sons caught the horse but disturbed Kapila, who was so annoyed that he instantly burnt them to ash with his fiery gaze.

When Sagara heard the story, he sent his grandson Ansuman to undo the harm. Ansuman descended to the underworld and met Kapila, who liked the maturity of the young man. He granted that the souls of the sixty thousand sons could be released by the waters of the goddess Ganga, who lived in heaven. Ganga agreed to come down to Earth. Although the impact of her watery fall would be severe, it could be softened by the god Shiva.

Finally, the river came down and fell into Shiva's matted hair, and then to Earth. This occurred at Gangotri. When the river located the ashes of the sixty thousand dead sons, the healing water brought them back to life and an ocean formed from the waters there, which became the Bay of Bengal.

newly married couples as well as newborn children. Bathing in the river—and gathering earthen pots full of it—as close to its source as possible was the lifelong quest of many Hindus. Annually, hearty young Hindus struggled up the mountains past the river's cascades to the Gangotri Glacier to bathe in and gather its holy water.

Devout Hindus incapable of climbing to the holy Gangotri Glacier could still receive the benefits of the river's sacred waters at sites along the river called *tirthas,* which were designated as holy sites. Three of the major sites designated by ancient Hindu priests are located along the Gangetic Plain at the cities of Hardwar, Allahabad, and Varanasi, and each attracted pilgrims for different reasons.

Hardwar is where the Ganges meets the plains after its precipitous descent from its glacial origins. Early Hindu pilgrims even traveled all the way from China to fill their earthen urns with the water at Hardwar. One such traveler described the city as: "Twenty *li* [3.5 miles] in circuit. The inhabitants are very numerous, and the pure streams of the river flow around on every side. There are always hundreds and thousands of people gathered together here from distant quarters to bathe and wash in its waters."[11] A sixteenth-century historian recorded the importance of Hardwar's water to the great Indian king Ali Akbar:

> His majesty calls this source of life the water of immortality. . . . Both at home and on his travels, he drinks the Ganges water. Trustworthy persons stationed on the banks of the river dispatch the water in sealed jars . . . . Now that his majesty is in the Punjab, water is brought from Hardwar.[12]

The second *tirtha* is the holy city of Allahabad, at the sacred confluence of the Ganges and the Yamuna Rivers. The confluence, known as the *sangam*, is considered to have great soul-cleansing and sin-wiping powers, thus making it a popular pilgrimage center. Allahabad, once named Prayag, was poetically described by Indian poet Kalidasa

in the fourth century A.D. The poet echoed the emotions of pilgrims journeying to this great joining of rivers:

A woman offers prayers at the Kumbha Mela celebration in Allahabad.

> When the water of the Ganges and the water of the Yamuna mingle, it appears as though diamonds and sapphires were woven together in a string; as though a flock of white swans had suddenly run into another flock of black swans; as though a garland of white lotus buds were interspersed with blue lotuses; as though streaks of lightning had merged into a sheet of darkness; as though a clear blue sky was spotted with wooly clouds of autumn.[13]

More than the other two *tirthas*, Allahabad was the favorite destination of early pilgrims taking part in a celebration called the Kumbha Mela, which occurred every twelve years. Even two thousand years ago, the city was mobbed by millions of Hindus for this one-day festival.

Kumbha Mela—Royal Bathing Day

Hinduism is rich with religious celebrations, but none is grander or celebrated by more people than the festival Kumbha Mela, which is held every twelve years on the banks of the Ganges River. This one-day celebration is marked by bathing in the holy river. The Kumbha Mela derives its name from the immortalizing pot of nectar described in India's ancient scriptures. *Kumbha* in the Sanskrit language means "pot," "pitcher," or "jar," and *Mela* means "festival." The Kumbha Mela is internationally famous as the largest gathering of human beings anywhere.

Although the celebration rotates each twelve years among the three *prayags*, the celebration at Allahabad is most renowned. On January 24, 2001, the Kumbha Mela was held in Allahabad, attracting an estimated 30 million bathers who prayed and took their holy dip in the river. Hindu priests proclaimed the Royal Bathing Day to begin at 3:20 P.M. on January 24 and to end

The last *tirtha* on the Ganges was the ancient city of Banares, modern-day Varanasi. Along the river in Varanasi, long stone stairways known as ghats were built providing safe access to the water. From the earliest times, millions of pilgrims trekked to the city for prayer and bathing. For those approaching the end of life, there could be no better place to die and be cremated.

Even for the dead, the miraculous power of the Ganges remained with them. For Hindus, nothing could be holier than dying by the banks of the Ganges, and if that was not possible, having one's ashes strewn on its waters. From India's leaders to ordinary citizens, the last rites of millions of Hindus have taken place in Varanasi. Typically, the body is cremated on one of many ghats along the riverbank, and the ashes cast into the river. According to the tenets of Hinduism, the immersion or scattering of ashes on the sacred river helps ensure the soul's journey toward eternal consciousness as well as salvation.

the next day. Although one day is designated as the Royal Bathing Day, the festival extends for forty-three days.

Eager to pray and wash away their sins in the river that Hindus consider their holiest site, worshipers dipped themselves in the water, which they scooped with hands and poured over their heads. They believe the ritual will wash away sins and answer prayers if performed at the auspicious time which occurs only once every four years. The believers seek salvation and a release from reincarnation to allow their spirits to move on to another life. The poor ask for riches, failed businessmen ask for success, and childless couples seek children as a gift from the river.

Although the focus of the celebration is spiritual, Allahabad also has all the sights, sounds, and smells of a massive party. Hotel and restaurant owners raise prices and make a quick profit from the crowds of pilgrims. Town merchants sell everything imaginable: food, toys, musical instruments, cassettes of holy music, and even tires and cellular telephones.

From birth to death, then, the dominant force in the lives of ancient Indians was the Ganges. Their respect was a reflection of a simple appreciation for the water that mysteriously sustained their lives and their faith that its abundant gift would never cease. The simple uses of the river for their agrarian and spiritual lives were not destined to last forever.

3

....

Harnessing the Ganges

The ancient rhythm of life along the Ganges was changed completely in the late seventeenth century with the arrival of Europeans. Industrialists from several European countries, most notably England, France, Denmark, and Holland, built factories in their homelands to produce large volumes of goods—mostly textiles—for hefty profits. To speed production and reduce costs, these industrialists built machines driven by steam engines and water wheels.

The main problem faced by these foreign entrepreneurs was providing enough raw materials to keep their machines running twenty-four hours a day. Europe lacked the proper climate to produce cotton, which forced manufacturers of textiles to look elsewhere for their raw material. The Ganges Basin was of interest to Europeans because of its favorable climate to grow cotton and because of the availability of plenty of water for nurturing crops. Initially, the industrialists confined their activities to buying cotton and some grain from farmers along the Gangetic Plain. Over time, however, England's booming industries dictated the harnessing of this seemingly limitless supply of water to increase crop production and to act as a disposal system for the chemical residues of a few new small factories.

The British and European industrialists who bought India's cotton faced significant competition, however. Visitors to India were impressed by the sophistication and skill of the local craftspeople, by their range of products, and by their well-organized and controlled small-scale cottage industries. Although Indian clothing was manufactured by hand, unlike machine-made European clothing, the Indian products were so popular that they transformed European fashion.

The owners of several British textile companies viewed Indian products as being too popular. Handsome profits were to be made manufacturing clothing and to the extent that the Indians were successful, British textile manufacturers would suffer. To limit competition from Indians,

The British East India Trading Company (illustrated below) transformed India's cotton industry.

Britain began to impose trade barriers and place high taxes on imported Indian-manufactured clothing. Gradually, India was forced to cease exporting manufactured cotton products in favor of exporting only raw cotton that British textile factories would then use for clothing. India's domestic textile industry declined as a result.

By 1840, British economic policies had reduced India to the status of a cotton supplier. Owners of the world's largest trading company, the British East India Trading Company, boasted, "encouraged and assisted by our great manufacturing ingenuity and skill, [we have] succeeded in converting India from a manufacturing country into a country exporting raw produce."[14] It was now time to dispatch freighters to the Ganges to ferry this bounty back to Britain.

Steamboats on the Ganges

Nothing symbolized the British presence in the Ganges Basin more than the steamboat. In fact, one of the advantages of the Ganges as far as the British were concerned was that the river was sufficiently large to be navigable by ships capable of carrying tons of cotton. The steamship would soon prove to be the link between the Ganges Basin and textile factories that drove Britain's industrial revolution.

Years before they succeeded in driving India out of the textile business, the British had foreseen the need for steamboats, and had enlisted the U.S. inventor Robert Fulton, the first to develop an efficient steamboat, to produce steam-powered vessels for use on the Ganges. Fulton entered an agreement with several British companies to provide steamboats for the Ganges; in a letter to Thomas Law, a British financier, dated April 16, 1812, Fulton said:

> I agree to make the Ganges enterprise a joint concern. You will please to send me a plan how you mean to proceed to secure a grant for 20 years and find funds to establish the first boats. It is so grand

an Idea that Americans should establish steam vessels to work in India that it requires vigor, activity, exertion, industry, attention, and that no time should be lost. My Paragon [a steamboat] beats everything on the globe...this Day she came in from Albany 160 miles in 26 hours, wind ahead....Keep the Ganges Secret.[15]

In addition to transporting Indian cotton and other products in larger quantities and at faster speeds than ships under sail could, steamboats revolutionized travel in the Ganges Basin. Before the arrival of the steamships, travelers and merchants in India were forced to use the old cumbersome methods of horseback, covered litters carried by runners, or rickety coaches rattling down rutted dirt roads. Steamboats became popular in the towns and cities along the Ganges as the most reliable and

The introduction of the steamboat revolutionized both trade and passenger travel along the Ganges River.

quickest form of passenger travel. Historian Henry Bernstein goes further, observing that the steamboat was the key to the colonial aspirations of the British, and not just in India.

> Of the many devices and processes that Europeans used to penetrate and conquer their Asian and African empires in the nineteenth century, the earliest to appear was the steamboat. It is doubtful that Europeans could have penetrated the continent so fast or dominated it so thoroughly if they had had to do so on foot.[16]

The British were not the only ones to benefit from the steamboats, however. Local merchants employed by British shipping firms as agents and representatives used their local knowledge to negotiate the buying and selling of cotton. Moreover, local people were themselves transformed by the cotton trade as a new merchant class grew wealthy from the commerce along the Ganges. In addition to serving as agents, local entrepreneurs organized steamer companies of their own. Their successes were a secondary benefit of the British commercial presence in the basin.

Dams

Once the Ganges Basin had become the center for cotton production and trade, the British dispatched engineers and hydrologists to study how they might harness the river to increase cotton production. British experts recognized that annual monsoon rains limited farmers to only a single crop of cotton and grain each year—not enough to satisfy the needs of British industry. The answer to this problem was irrigation projects, which required damming the river.

Dams increased cotton and grain production by enabling farmers to irrigate with excess water captured during the monsoon season and stored in reservoirs. The stored water could then be released as needed during the dry season, providing at least two crops each year. In some areas, cotton and wheat were alternated under what was called cotton-wheat double cropping. Under this arrangement, cotton was planted in the spring and picked in late fall. Immediately following the picking, winter wheat was planted and then harvested in the spring.

The reservoirs were expected to store enough water to allow for the irrigation of areas far from the river, which were normally too dry for farming. Such a network of dams and canals would bring to life millions of new acres of formerly useless land.

One problem with this plan was that damming the Ganges itself would block the steamships that were so vital to the region's prosperity. To solve this problem British engineers designed and constructed several successful earth and concrete dams on tributaries of the Ganges. Each dam was capable of storing from 10 to 30 billion cubic feet of water. These reservoirs were small by comparison with reservoirs elsewhere in the world, with capacities of several trillion cubic feet; still, they made a significant contribution to the region's agricultural productivity.

With the completion of each dam, more water that might otherwise have flooded land was instead stored and made available for irrigation during the drought season. Controlling the monsoon floods was an additional benefit of the dams. Abnormally heavy monsoon rains were destructive to farmers because they either prevented the timely planting of crops or washed away newly seeded fields. Heavy rains also were destructive in the Gangetic Plain where floodwaters could and often did wash away entire towns, drowning thousands of people in the process.

The first dams caused desert areas to bloom year-round. As the cool clear waters filled reservoirs and canals, and eventually saturated thirsty crops, agriculture flourished. For the first time, farmers along the Ganges who had previously barely fed themselves began to enjoy profits from their fields.

The Ganges Canal

Perhaps not surprisingly, a shift from an emphasis on small dams to larger and more ambitious alterations to the natural flow of the river began. In 1854, British engineers undertook their first large-scale disruption of the Ganges. Rather than continue building small dams, they identified a corridor of land between the Ganges and Yamuna Rivers as a prime candidate for irrigation. A team led by British engineer Proby Cautley determined that a large canal running down the center of the region between the two rivers could provide water for several million acres of farmland.

The British government was happy to fund the project because it understood that the more cotton British textile mills imported, the more tax money the government would receive from the sale of finished goods. As one person involved in a later extension of the canal observed, "It is very certain that if the restoration and extension of these works [Ganges Canal] had not promised an increase of revenue to the British Government, they would not have been undertaken."[17]

The British understood that crops produced in this region would then require transportation thirteen hundred miles east to the port of Calcutta, where British ships would then transport them to Britain. Trains at this time were a new form of transportation, and the building of rail lines across India was a daunting and expensive undertaking that no one wanted to tackle. Instead, the decision was made that any canal would be designed to double for both irrigation and for shipping. To accommodate steamboats, Cautley designed the concrete-lined canal to be 150 feet wide and 16 feet deep. Despite the enormity of the project, such a design represented a considerable cost savings to the British.

The British hoped the canal would transform a parched land where few crops could survive into vast stretches of white cotton bolls. The British motivation, however, was not entirely self-serving. The government was also aware

British Imperialism

British manufacturers made inroads into India and other countries during the eighteenth century in search of the raw materials needed for their factories. Many justified their actions by claiming that their entry and eventual economic and political dominance of their colonies was justified by the Bible and by British moral superiority. Historian Daniel R. Headrick wrote an article for the Journal of Modern History *in June 1979 called, "The Tools of Imperialism: Technology and the Expansion of European Colonial Empires in the Nineteenth Century," in which he discussed the imperialistic views of British entrepreneur Macgregor Laird.*

His self-proclaimed motives were a mixture of philanthropy, Christianity, and profit, as he once said: "to create new and extensive markets for our manufactured goods, and fresh sources whence to draw our supplies;...to raise their fellow creatures from their present degraded, denationalized and demoralized state nearer to Him in whose image they were created."

Yet this son of a shipbuilder was also as much an enthusiast for technical progress as for business and religion:

We have the power in our hands, moral, physical and mechanical—the first, based on the Bible; the second, upon the wonderful adaptation of the Anglo-Saxon race to all climates, situations, and circumstances...the third, bequeathed to us by the immortal Watt [inventor of the steam engine]. By his invention every river is laid open to us, time and distance are shortened. If his spirit is allowed to witness the success of his invention here on earth, I can conceive no application of it that would receive his approbation more than seeing the mighty streams of the Mississippi and the Amazon, the Niger and the Nile, the Indus and the Ganges, stemmed by hundreds of steam-vessels, carrying the glad tidings of "peace and good will toward men" into the dark places of the earth which are now filled with cruelty.

that famine occasionally visited misery on communities throughout the Ganges Basin. Severe droughts between 1837–1839 and 1845–1852 had led to starvation that killed tens of thousands of Indians. One condition placed on the construction of a canal, therefore, was that in addition to cotton, food crops such as grains, nuts, and vegetables also had to be grown. Richard Baird Smith, one of the lead engineers commented, "This great tract will become the garden of the North Western Provinces; and we shall hear no more of those devastating famines, which have hitherto swept across it."[18]

Construction on the canal and diversion dam at Hardwar began in 1848 and the job was completed downstream at Allahabad in 1854. The volume of water diverted from the Ganges was fixed at 6,750 cubic feet per second (cusec). Calculations performed by agronomists indicated that one cusec would irrigate 654 acres and that the entire canal would irrigate almost 4.4 million acres. In 1865, the canal was extended to a total of 181 miles southeast with numerous branches accounting for another 2,266 miles.

Modern Irrigation

Over the decades that followed the canal's construction, a network of smaller waterways was gradually developed. As the Ganges flows into Hardwar, the dam diverts its allotment down the concrete canal. As the water flows down it, hundreds of smaller perpendicular branches carry the water for many miles on either side of the main channel. Sluice gates allow water to flow from the concrete canals to smaller dirt channels into which farmers inserted siphons to suck the water to their rows of crops. The tapping of water was carefully regulated to maintain sufficient depth in the canal for steamboats and to guarantee sufficient water for farmers whose land was farthest from Hardwar.

Each farmer was allowed the same amount of water per acre, which was measured by a simple timing device made of brass. This device consisted of a small bowl with a pin-sized hole in the bottom. The official timer opened the sluice gate and as he did, he placed the brass timing bowl into a bucket of water. When the bowl filled with water and sank, the timer closed the sluice gate. Anyone

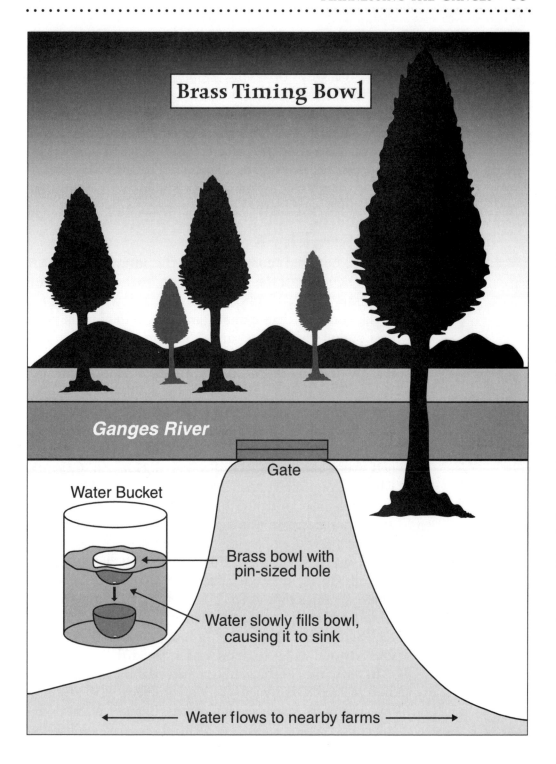

Brass Timing Bowl

Ganges River

Gate

Water Bucket

Brass bowl with
pin-sized hole

Water slowly fills bowl,
causing it to sink

← Water flows to nearby farms →

caught taking more water than his share or attempting to bribe the timekeeper was subject to severe punishment.

The Ganges Canal was an immediate unqualified success from nearly everyone's point of view. It dramatically increased crop production, pleasing the British industrialists who needed the cotton as well as the farmers along the Ganges who grew it. As the Ganges' water irrigated more cropland, larger boats were required to carry the flow of raw materials on the long trip to Britain and more people found jobs keeping the boats and their cargo moving.

The Farakka Barrage

For one hundred years following the advent of commercial agriculture in the Ganges Basin, boatloads of cotton and grain steamed without interruption down the Ganges to the port of Calcutta and from there to the British ports of London, Liverpool, and Southampton. Rarely had greater progress been made with less apparent impact on the natural environment. With the exception of the Ganges Canal and a few dams, little more was done to alter the natural course of the Ganges.

By the 1950s, however, the large forty-thousand-ton oceangoing freighters that were hauling agricultural products were experiencing difficulties docking at Calcutta, which is connected to the Ganges and the Bay of Bengal by the Hugli (also Hooghly) River. The silt carried downriver and deposited there was making the river so shallow that freighters could no longer reach the docks. Although the Hugli was not the only tributary to experience serious deposits of silt, it received the lion's share of the Ganges' total—a staggering 4.75 billion tons of silt annually. Despite efforts to dredge the Hugli, large ships were running aground. The economy of India's second most populous city and its busiest port was in jeopardy.

In the early 1960s, engineers surveyed the clogged river and proposed a remedy to the problem. The solution involved periodically sending a large burst of water down the river, creating enough of a current to drive millions of

The Bridge of Boats

Crossing the Ganges has never been a simple task. Although a few bridges now exist in large cities, before they were built people crossed in small boats or found places where large rocks protruded above the low waters during the dry season. One group of villagers, however, weary of the uncertainties of crossing the river, devised a clever plan for spanning it.

At a point on the river that is less than one mile wide during the monsoon and only three-tenths of a mile during the dry months, villagers constructed a bridge of boats. The boats used were small, measuring ten feet long and four feet wide. Hundreds were tied together side by side, from one bank of the river to the other. When the boats were in place, ropes anchored them to large trees on each side of the river to prevent them from drifting downstream.

Next, carts full of wood and straw were layered across the boats to create a roadway for foot traffic. A fee was charged to each person wishing to use the bridge. If large boats wished to pass the bridge, a fee was charged to the captain for the removal of a center section until the boat passed. Small boats were lifted from the river and dragged around the bridge of boats. The bridge of boats attracted many travelers, which spawned a marketplace where goods for travelers were sold.

tons of silt far out into the Bay of Bengal. Engineers calculated that if they could divert forty thousand cusec of water down the Hugli in bursts, the force would be sufficient to remove the silt and reopen the docks. To find such a volume of water, engineers looked upriver to a point in the Ganges just before it branches out into the hundreds of streams that weave their way through the Delta.

In 1971, a location on the Ganges near India's border with Bangladesh was chosen to erect a great concrete dam to divert water away from the Delta's many small streams and down the Hugli instead. A dam of this sort, intended exclusively for the diversion of water, is called by engineers a barrage; officials dubbed this dam the Farakka

Barrage. By 1975, the nine-thousand-foot-long concrete barrage near the city of Bihar was in full operation. To the delight of all concerned, the burst flushing—combined with continued dredging—was successful and the port of Calcutta was once again open to large ships.

Industrial Growth on the Ganges

At the same time British textile manufacturers were prospering, many Indians were thriving economically as well. The colonial strategy of forcing the Indians to sell and trade agricultural products such as cotton and grain rather than processing them into manufactured products had not applied to all facets of the Indian economy. Through the nineteenth and well into the twentieth centuries, although agriculture remained the heart of the Ganges economy, Indians were able to develop other industries that did not conflict with the aggressive aims of the British industrialists.

Indian entrepreneurs took advantage of the opportunity to make profits in many industries such as leather tanning, chemical plants, sugar processing, and synthetic fertilizer production. The populations along the river viewed industries such as these as economic saviors because they offered jobs to urban dwellers and offered some struggling farmers an alternative to working small unprofitable plots of land.

Of all the industries that grew up in the Ganges Basin, the largest was tanning. Although Hinduism teaches that cattle are sacred, once the animals die their hides can be used without violating religious doctrine. The Ganges Basin is home to a significant percentage of the tanneries because these facilities must be built on a large river capable of carrying off the chemical residues from the tanning process.

Meanwhile, sugar processing became a major industry along the Ganges. Sugarcane had grown in abundance along the Ganges for more than twenty-five hundred years but irrigation greatly increased the amount of sugar-

A man prepares cattle hides in a Ganges Basin tannery.

cane produced, and modern techniques for extracting and purifying sugar allowed India to become a major exporter of sugar. Over time, factories expanded by hiring thousands of workers. Towns grew up that were completely dependent on sugar production for jobs. As was true of tanneries, sugar processing plants used the river to carry away chemical residues from the refining processes.

A Natural Kidney?

Hindus have always revered the sanctity of the Ganges' water as being capable of spiritual cleansing as well as healing the body. Regardless of the river's pollution, faithful Hindus have always believed that the water was able to miraculously maintain its purity.

In the 1930s, an interesting observation was made. People noticed that the domestic wastewater from Calcutta could be used as an alternative source of water for the fish farms. Regardless of the concentration of the polluted wastewater, when it was siphoned into ponds, the fish thrived in it. Local fish farmers tested the water and found that it contained almost no organic waste, making it nearly as pure as well water.

No one in the scientific community paid any attention to this seemingly miraculous phenomenon until it was reported to Professor D.S. Bhargava, an environmental engineer at the University of Roorkee. In 1980, Bhargava conducted studies in collaboration with the Indian Institute of Technology in Kanpur by monitoring water at various locations along the river at different seasons over a five-year period. Following his studies, Bhargava reported in a technical paper that the Ganges was indeed able to purify its own water, stating that the river was able to decompose organic waste fifteen to twenty-five times faster than other rivers. Faculty at the institute in Kanpur proclaimed that the river functioned like a natural kidney in the way it filtered its own water.

Bhargava tested the river rather than the fishponds where the reported miraculous purification occurred. His findings, however, have never been fully explained, yet devout Hindus have always pointed to his study as proof of the river's mystical powers of purity as stated in the *Veda*.

More recently, however, scientists have discredited Bhargava's study. They explain that there is no evidence for the "natural kidney" phenomenon. They further pointed out that the cleansing of the fishpond water was the result of bacteria acting to decompose the organic matter in the sewage. The scientists concluded that the pond bacteria were, in reality, the so-called natural kidney, but that it would not be effective for cleaning up the river.

As the output of both raw and processed agricultural products increased, the Ganges farmers and industry owners sought ways to increase production and profits still further. The river was providing adequate water, but farmers realized that to increase production they would have to supplement natural nutrients with chemical fertilizers. Agronomists and chemists developed synthetic fertilizers using ammonia, phosphorus, chlorine, potassium, and of course, water from the Ganges. In the middle of the twentieth century, manufacturers built plants along the Ganges to produce fertilizer.

By the 1980s, thousands of workers were annually producing thousands of tons of fertilizer, further boosting the economy of the Ganges Basin. The production of chemical fertilizers spawned yet more industries: mining operations to extract chemicals needed for producing the fertilizers; trucking, railroad, and steamship companies to transport the millions of tons of raw materials; and packaging companies to box and wrap the end products.

The harnessing of the river through the construction of dams and a web of canals propelled the economy of the Ganges Basin. Indian farmers and small factory owners along the Ganges experienced a rise in their standard of living as did almost everyone else involved, in one way or another, with the economy of the river. Yet, there were signs of trouble. Devout Hindus and others who continued bathing in the Ganges on a daily basis were noticing skin rashes and sores. The water that Hindu believers held was pure as it had been for thousands of years was not. Obviously, the Ganges was paying the price of prosperity.

4

· · · · · · · · · ·

A River in Distress

By the 1970s, what had once appeared to be a limitless supply of sparkling freshwater was gradually but noticeably acquiring the look and smell of a dying river. As scientists began closely examining the Ganges, they discovered what local populations had known for years: The water quality had markedly declined, allowing diseases to proliferate among local people and wildlife.

The Ganges Basin had dramatically changed from what it had been one hundred years earlier when farms were still small, when the population was one-quarter of its current total, and when few industries occupied the banks of the river.

Today, the major sources of pollution along the Ganges are the estimated six thousand factories on the river, especially the leather factories, which produce dozens of highly toxic chemicals that are dumped into the river. The second-worst source of pollution is the untreated raw sewage that daily enters the river. The third is the Hindus' ritual use of the Ganges as a sacred burial place. Annually, millions of cremated and partially cremated bodies are committed to the river.

The Population Curse

Despite the best intentions of everyone living along the Ganges of respecting the river, an exploding population makes fulfilling those intentions impossible. The improved economy along the Ganges resulting from increased crop and industrial production has been accompanied by an equally dramatic increase in population. Demographers point out that the population of the Ganges Basin was 100 million in 1900 but today it is 400 million and climbing.

At the heart of the population boom is improved health care. As the region prospered, money was designated for building hospitals and clinics. Children received inoculations against common childhood diseases such as measles, cholera, and smallpox that before had killed thousands. Older people too lived healthier, longer lives. They began receiving improved medical care that extended the average

A Hindu cremation. Each year millions of bodies are cremated along the Ganges River.

life span from forty-two years in 1900 to fifty-seven today.

Improved health care was a friend to the people of the Ganges but an enemy to the river. Ballooning populations have stressed the river as more raw sewage pours into it. Pollution of the Ganges has become the most serious threat to the river and all who depend on its waters. So degraded is the quality of the water that the religious ritual of bathing in the Ganges has become a health hazard.

Bathing with the Dead

It is estimated that 10 million people bathe in the Ganges daily and that most Hindus, who make up over 80 percent of India's more than 1 billion people, will undertake a pilgrimage to the Ganges at least once in their lives. Hindus, however, believe that the Ganges has a role beyond purifying their spirits.

For the devout Hindu, the ideal end is for one's remains to be cremated and committed to *Ma Ganga*. In the presence of friends and family, the deceased is burned on a large wooden pyre placed along the Ganges, usually at one of the three tirthas. When the flames subside and the body has been reduced to ashes and bones, those in attendance gather the remains along with any unburned wood and cast everything into the river. The total number of annual cremations along the Ganges can only be estimated but the number may exceed 30 million annually. Indian health officials point to this volume of human ashes and partially burned wood as a significant source of pollution in the river.

A bigger problem that has recently arisen, however, is partial cremations due to the scarcity of wood. An effective pyre requires four hundred pounds of wood to reduce a body to ashes and costs about one hundred dollars, a considerable sum for most families. Some poor Hindu families resort to smaller pyres that only partially cremate a body; others simply slip their dead relatives into the river and watch them float downstream. D. Chakaraborti of the Central Ganges Authority commented on the problem created by partially cremated bodies: "When these bodies decompose, they pollute the water to a dangerous level."[19]

Compounding this problem are dead animals and people that are not required by Hindu tradition to be cremated. This group includes cattle, which are sacred to Hindus, children under twelve years old, and pregnant women. Because they are all considered embodiments of purity that do not need to be purified by cremation, these bodies are simply tied to a rock, rowed out into the middle of the river, and thrown overboard. Although most dead cattle are skinned and the hides used to produce leather, an estimated sixty thousand to eighty thousand are cast into the Ganges annually.

The carcass of a skinned cow is rolled into the Ganges.

Life at the Ghats

The central function of the ghats that line the banks of the Ganges as it flows through cities is to provide access to the holy water for bathers and for disposal of the dead. Observers who have visited them, however, report that they are much more than concrete stairs leading to the river.

Ghats come to life just before the sun rises, when a few pious worshipers arrive to cleanse themselves. Shortly after sunrise, kids frolic in the river, playing games with the tourist boats while their mothers wash clothes. At some ghats, women bathe at one end and men at the other. Following the ritual bath, many produce bars of soap and wash themselves. Men are permitted to strip down to a loincloth but women must be completely covered at all times, even when applying soap.

After the morning rush hour, vendors set up portable stoves on the ghats to sell food and tea. More pilgrims arrive to take holy baths side by side with women who have brought clay and iron pots in need of scrubbing before beginning the evening meal. This is also the most popular time for boats to cruise slowly by the ghats, allowing foreign tourists to photograph the activity found here.

Finally, as the sun goes down, the ghats attract people who come out to stroll along the promenade, to catch up on gossip, to have another wash, and to sit and watch people walk by. When darkness is complete, the lights come on and slowly people drift off to their homes, except for the hundreds of poor who regularly sleep on the ghats themselves.

The presence of decomposing bodies in the river poses a serious health risk and is of great concern to India's medical community. Patrick Fuller, a spokesperson for the International Red Cross, expressed fears that decaying bodies are contaminating drinking water, spreading cholera, gastroenteritis, hepatitis, and diarrhea.

Evidence clearly points to the dead as a significant source of pollution. Health officials testing the water one mile upriver from Hardwar found it comparatively pure, having a low Bio-Oxygen Demand (BOD), an indication of the amount of decaying organic matter in the water. (The more organic waste there is in the water, the more oxygen is needed by the microorganisms that decompose it and the higher the BOD.) Immediately downriver from Hardwar, however, the BOD skyrockets. In 1998, Dr. D.G. Thimmiah, a member of an agency called the Ganges Planning Commission, said that Hindus might not pollute the river as much if they did not worship it as much:

> The Ganga is no longer willing to wash out the sins of Hindus. They worship her, but they do not regret defecating all over her body. They have abused her so much that she has lost her life. We don't want Hindus to worship her, because then they will not pollute her with dead bodies.[20]

Raw Sewage

As a source of pollution of even greater significance than dead bodies is raw sewage flowing into the river. The Ganges' foul condition, which qualifies it as one of the world's most polluted rivers, is partially the result of having the highest population density of any major river. The Ganges flows through seven hundred cities and countless villages in India. As the river sweeps past each one, it receives the untreated wastes of all living there. One hundred years ago, when the Ganges Basin was home to an estimated 100 million people, the river was relatively effective at removing human waste with only marginal signs of contamination. Today, however, the river's population has quadrupled and Indian health officials estimate that the daily flow of raw sewage is slightly more than 250 million gallons.

In 2000, a report on the water quality of rivers around the world was released by the Water Policy and Planning Group Environmental Protection Department. The Ganges was tested, studied, and analyzed by scientists interested in determining its general health. The conclusion drawn by the researchers found the Ganges to be "either 'bad' or 'very bad' mainly due to pollution by livestock waste and from unsewered villages."[21]

With all this sewage pouring into the river, pathogens have increased dramatically. According to a report issued by doctors attending a meeting to study the illness of the Ganges, "In some places the fecal-coliform [a type of bacteria inhabiting the intestinal tracts of humans and animals] count has reached 170,000,000 bacteria per 100 ml. [milliliters] of water; a terrifying 34,000,000% greater than the acceptable level. It is no wonder why so many children die each year."[22] The fecal-coliform count is one way of measuring water quality; the lower the count, the cleaner the water. According to members of the Sankat Mochan Foundation, an organization that has

Raw sewage containing deadly pathogens pours into the waters of the Ganges.

been struggling to reverse the environmental degradation of the Ganges,

> Upstream from Varanasi, one of the major pilgrimage sites along the river, the water is comparatively pure, having a low Bio-Oxygen Demand (BOD) and [low] Fecal Coliform Count. However, once the river enters the city these levels rise alarmingly. Measurements taken at the city's various bathing ghats during a few years ago show that the average BOD of the water rises by over 1300 percent. The average Fecal Coliform Count at the ghats is over 6000 times what it is before the river enters the city.[23]

Industrial Pollution

As unsightly and dangerous pollution in the form of bloated bodies and sewage dumped daily into the Ganges might be, it is the chemical discharges by factories that are the more damaging. Even though municipal sewage constitutes 80 percent of the total volume of waste dumped into the Ganges while factories contribute about 15 percent, industrial waste has a far more destructive impact.

To illustrate the extent of the problem, in 1984 the Ganges caught fire near Barauni, the result of two chemical manufacturing plants and an oil refinery discharging flammable fluids into the river. Flames were reported to be twenty feet high and all efforts to extinguish the blaze failed. Finally, after sixteen hours, the fire burned itself out when the flammable fluids were consumed.

In the past seventy-five years, thousands of factories have been built along the Ganges. Tanneries, chemical plants, textile mills, distilleries, oil- and coal-fired electrical generating plants, and petroleum refineries discharge untreated chemically contaminated wastewater through a myriad of open drains and canals. Annually, factories along the Ganges dump an estimated 6 million tons of chemical fertilizers and nine thousand tons of pesticides into the river.

Of all the sources of pollution, scientists point to the 120 tanneries along the Ganges as the worst offenders. The most concentrated assault on the river occurs at the city of Kanpur, where eighty tanneries operate. The hides of horses, goats, and cattle are brought to the factories and during the tanning process, a large volume of effluent is discharged. The hides go through an extensive chemical treatment from the time they are scoured with lime to when they are treated with chromium salts and ammonium sulfide. The chromium salts, highly toxic chemicals, are present in such a high concentration that they impart a greenish hue to the city of Kanpur's drinking water, which is drawn from the river. Organic waste—hair, flesh, and other animal remains—are thrown into the river, giving it a rotten stench. As this offensive mix sinks into the water, it mingles with the effluents of other industrial plants such as sugar refineries that disgorge a thick molasses-like mix of organic and chemical residue.

The sugar industry, a major employer in India, uses a wide array of chemicals to refine granular sugar from sugarcane. The sugar refineries daily produce hundreds of tons using dizzying variety of chemicals such as wetting agents, acid inhibitors, juice clarification polymers, and defoaming agents. They also use a variety of chemicals to remove inorganic and organic deposits, ion exchange resins, and other chemicals from filters and bulk storage containers. The volume of chemical wastes from the sugar refineries is immense—equal to the amount of refined sugar piled along the river's wharves awaiting shipment.

The worst of the pollution enters the Ganges close to where it empties into the Bay of Bengal. Near the mouth of the Ganges 150 large industrial plants are lined up on the banks of one of the Ganges' tributaries, the Hugli at Calcutta. Together, these plants contribute 30 percent of the total industrial pollution reaching the mouth of the Ganges. Of this, half comes from pulp and paper industries, which discharge a dark brown, oxygen-craving slurry of bark and wood fiber. Other discharges include

mercury and other heavy metals, which accumulate in fish tissues, and chemical toxins like bleaches and dyes, which produce dioxin and other known cancer-causing agents. In the United States, the Environmental Protection Agency (EPA) has set a limit for these types of contaminants at one hundred particles per liter of water—the count in the Hugli, however, is over six thousand.

By-products of the tanning industry, which contain chemical and organic waste, flow freely into the Ganges.

A Dying Fish Industry

Because of chemical pollution and high levels of oxygen-consuming microorganisms, the Ganges has become a river of sickness and death for native fish. By 1970, pollution had greatly reduced the Ganges fishing industry to the extent that deputy director for Indian fisheries, K. Gopakumar proclaimed, "Pollution is one of the biggest killers of inland fish. And traditional fisherfolk are [the] worst affected."[24] The village of Tajpur, near the

Bangladesh border, as an example, once employed half of the city's population of two hundred adults in the fishing industry, but today only four fishermen still venture out into the river.

Data from the Central Inland Capture Fisheries Research Institute (CICFRI) confirms that fish catches along the Ganges are declining. Annual inland fish catches of major species of carp in the cities of Allahabad and Bhagalpur have drastically declined. At Allahabad, the carp catch in 1958 of ninety-three tons declined in 1998 to five tons and the *hilsa*—a type of salmon—for the same years declined from twenty tons to just two. The city of Bhagalpur experienced similar declines of catch.

Tons of fish that might once have been hauled aboard fishing boats are now found floating along riverbanks in what are termed "mass fish deaths" in which tens of thousands of fish wash ashore in one large heap. Ichthyologists, biologists specializing in the study of fish, have discovered that fish deaths are of two types depending upon whether pollution is the result of organic or inorganic effluents. Each of these two categories of pollutants causes a particular form of sickness and death in fish.

Organic pollution, primarily from human waste and animal and human remains, causes the indirect death of fish. Fish do not die from ingesting human excrement and decaying bodies themselves; rather they succumb to the loss of oxygen in the water that accompanies high concentrations of such organic matter. When organic matter decays, it is broken down into smaller organic molecules by a variety of enzymes secreted by naturally occurring bacteria. Consumed in the decay process is oxygen that is dissolved in the water and which fish must have in order to survive. An indication of the river's condition is that a single gallon of highly polluted Ganges water tested down-river from Hardwar contained 6.8 billion bacteria.

The second major cause of fish deaths is poisoning from ingestion of inorganic chemical toxins. Pharmaceutical companies in Hardwar, tanneries in Kanpur, and

"We Will Fight till Death, We Are Dying Anyway"

In 2002, reporter S.S. Jeevan visited a Ganges fishing village to report on the impoverished lives of fishermen suffering from declining fish stocks, which have led to various forms of illegal fishing. His report "Orphans of the River" was published in the February 15, 2002 periodical Down to Earth.

At the age of 50, Phekia Devi has seen the transition of her fellow fisherfolk: from the days of oppression of the landlords to the betrayal by their own people. As she walks on the banks of the Ganga, she describes how the fishing mafia stripped her folks of their livelihood. She talks of the time when they had fish, when they used to help their men carrying the big *rohu* and *katla*. She also narrates how they managed to free themselves from the clutches of the feudal lords. The times when she was arrested, the times she sat on *dharnas* [prayer meetings]. It was a fierce struggle, [but] she would say "We

were determined to be free or die."

With a dwindling fish population, people have resorted to devious methods to catch fish. In Bihar, rich contractors are known to poison the river at one point and collect the dead fish that are available. "About 100 grammes of *parmar* (aldrin) can kill fish for up to 3 km. It does not even spare the eggs and the living organisms the fish depends on," says Gangaram Sadha of Deoka village, Madhubani. "The use of dynamite sticks to blow up a portion of the river is also a common practice in many rivers."

Always on her toes, Devi takes you anywhere you want to go. The goons and illegal fishers, though wary of her presence, quietly walk away. They know better than to cross her fiery attitude and mouth. After narrating the plight of the fisherfolk, she asks: "You have seen our problems. Will you be able to help?" She has lost hope in the government. But she stands firm: "We will fight till death. We are dying anyway."

synthetic fertilizer plants in Agra repeatedly ravage the Ganges with the release of toxic substances such as cadmium, chromium, lead, and acetone. These toxins annually poison thousands of tons of fish. As a result, according to Ashok Bishaya, a prominent member of the

Ganges fishing community, "Five species of fish that used to be abundant are now rare."[25]

In the early 1990s, ichthyologists proposed to study the effects of the river's pollution on fish. They raised native fish in clean pools, placed the fish in large mesh cages, and then lowered them into the Ganges at locations known to have high concentrations of pollutants. According to a report by the Center for Science and the Environment in New Delhi, at one location immediately downstream from several paper and pulp mills and a sugar refinery, the immersed cage of fish survived only five hours. A short distance downstream from Barauni, at the point where waste from the Bata shoe factory mixes with oil from a refinery, the fish fared little better, surviving only eight hours.

Problems with Dams

Scientists studying the distress of the Ganges agree that the many sources of pollution are the worst of the river's problems. Yet, pollution is not the sole cause of distress for the river. Limnologists point to dams as another cause for concern. The Ganges has only two major dams, one at Hardwar and the other at Farakka, however, dozens of smaller dams are built on its many tributaries. The purpose of every dam in the Ganges Basin is either to divert water to other tributaries and canals or to control flooding during unusually severe monsoon rains and later to release the water for crop irrigation during the dry season. Although the river basin's array of dams is small by comparison with other major rivers, it is, nonetheless, one of the sources of problems along this majestic river.

Prior to the construction of dams, one of the ways the Ganges was once able to carry off pollutants yet remain relatively healthy for human and fish populations was by continually purging itself. Fresh infusions of water from monsoon rains and from its many tributaries high in the Himalayas flushed pollutants downstream rather than letting them settle to the bottom. With the construction of dams, the volume of water and the speed with which it flows as it moves across the Gangetic and Delta zones has been reduced. Water diverted down the Ganges Canal, water held in check at the Farakka Barrage, and water stored behind dozens of small dams has dramatically reduced the force of the river's flow and its flushing capacity.

Dams are also the enemy of fish. Dams not only prevent the normal cleansing process of the river but also block the routes of migratory fish that travel upriver to spawn. According to R.K. Sinha, of Patna University, "The Ganges Canal dam at Hardwar and the Farakka barrage in Bihar that came up in 1975 have made a deep impact on the fish catch. Around 98 percent of the fishery has collapsed."[26] The damming of the Ganges has also deeply affected fish diversity. According to P.K. Mishra, "The situation [of dams] is grim. Commercial species of fish in many stretches of the Ganges has dwindled from 183 species in 1955 to just 43 in 1992."[27]

The Suffering Delta

The Delta is the unfortunate recipient of all the ills of the Ganges. The water quality of the river declines significantly along its course to the sea to such a degree that by the time it reaches the Delta, it is a river of filth. The Delta zone, which represents only 13 percent of the Ganges' length, is subjected to 100 percent of the river's pollution. This zone has suffered more environmental degradation than the others in terms of habitat destruction. Crustaceans, which by their nature inhabit the ocean floor where much of the particulate pollutants settle, are most affected. The floor of the river is also the place where toxic metals such as mercury, arsenic, and chromium from the tanneries and chemical factories further upriver accumulate. Furthermore, when crustaceans such as crabs, shrimp, lobster, and other small marine animals ingest pollutants, those chemicals enter the food chain and are passed along to all animals that feed on the crustaceans, including humans.

The reduced flow of the Ganges, a direct result of the Farakka Barrage, has caused a build-up of garbage along the shores of the river.

The problem of pollutants is compounded by the presence of the two large and several small dams along the Gangetic Plain that reduce the rivers' force by the time it enters the Delta. Until 1975, the Delta relied on the purging action of the Ganges' powerful flow during the monsoon season to flush pollutants from the river. However, with the completion of the Farakka Barrage, the flushing action ceased. Although the barrage directs some flushing action down the Hugli to keep Calcutta's harbor clear, the effect throughout much of the Delta is that higher concentrations of pollutants build up over time.

The Delta has suffered a similar problem with salt pollution from the ocean. Without the flushing action of the river, increased salt concentrations have caused additional wildlife deaths. According to A.H.M. Ali Reza, a zoologist from the University of Jahangirnagar in Dhaka, Bangladesh, the damming of the Ganges is the primary

The Endangered Bengal Tiger

No one will debate the fact that the Bengal tiger is a man-eater. Dozens of Indian and Bangladesh fishermen and farmers are eaten annually by the big cats. What will generate debate, however, among local villagers who fear the tiger, and zoologists who seek to study and preserve the endangered orange-and-black-striped predator, is why humans are eaten and how to prevent further loss of life.

Zoologists are quick to point out that the natural habitat for these immense tigers is the Delta zone of the Ganges near the Bay of Bengal. Because the human population has increased over past decades along with the toxic pollutants in the water, the tigers are finding less food to eat. As the decline of its natural prey continues, tigers are forced to find alternate species to eat. The most prolific animal species now living in the Delta, and the only one with an expanding population, is *Homo Sapiens*.

Zoologist A.H.M. Ali Reza, who reported on the tiger on ENN's website, believes the man-eating behavior is more complicated than the tiger simply seeing humans as an easy source of food. Dr. Ali Reza reported that, "Researchers believe that the tigers get their taste for human flesh primarily from the half-burnt bodies that make their way down the sacred Ganges River. Upstream in India, funeral pyres are lit on the banks of the Ganges and the bodies thrown into the river for their journey into the next world." Cleaning the corpses from the river, he concluded, may prevent young tigers from acquiring a taste for human flesh.

Reza's report is of little consolation to local villagers. In the same ENN story, Charles Santiapillai, a Sri Lankan zoologist, stated, "The tigers are extremely bold here. They will carry off fishermen napping in their boats or stalk villagers who have come to collect firewood."

The current challenge for conservationists and villagers is to set aside areas that are more isolated for the tiger and its natural prey. Such a solution will require compromise and commitment on both sides, but similar preserves for endangered animals have been successful in other countries.

cause for loss of wildlife species in the Delta, all the way up to the top of the food chain:

> Due to . . . the damming of a river that once fed the wetlands, salinity in the Sundarbans [the Delta] has increased. Even species such as barking deer and hog deer are no longer seen in the swamp. As a result, the tiger often goes hungry, stalking rhesus monkey and wild boar when spotted deer are scarce.[28]

Critics of the Farakka Barrage, primarily the government of Bangladesh, also blame its existence for causing thousands of human drowning deaths in the Delta. Before the barrage, when the Delta naturally flooded during the monsoon season, its population was able to escape to high ground or to survive in their homes built on tall poles. Following the construction of the barrage, however, India now periodically opens the sluice gates, adding billions of gallons of stored water to the normal floodwaters. Critics argue that the combination of stored water and floodwaters released in a sudden torrent are partially responsible for drowning deaths each year. In the flood of 1991, 150,000 people perished beneath the floodwaters.

Tourism

At the Ganges source, where waters are the purest and the population sparse, Hindu faithful and mountain trekkers seek spiritual guidance and solitude. Unfortunately for the Ganges, this area has experienced the most dramatic rise in popularity of the three zones. A 2001 study by the Indian Mountaineering Foundation arrived at the astonishing conclusion that Gangotri Glacier is the most popular destination for tourists in India. This holy location, which accounts for the first ten miles of the Ganges, annually attracts over 250,000 Hindu pilgrims, 15 to 20,000 trekkers, and over a thousand expeditions attempting to climb the nearby peaks.

The effect of this influx of people on a tiny place like Gangotri has been an ecological disaster. As the number of tourists grew, so did their demands for comfort. To meet the demands, traditional footpaths became roads for cars, serene hillsides became sites of hotels and restaurants, and the alpine forests became the firewood that heats the hotels and cooks food. The destruction of the high-altitude juniper and silver birch forests is a natural consequence of the demand to provide heat for so many visitors. As the fires warm rooms, the ash falls in the river adding to the particulate wastes cascading down the mountain. Garbage and human waste are regularly dumped into what was once the pristine source of this sacred river.

What might be even worse than the proliferation of hotels and restaurants is the recent construction of the airport at Lukla, Nepal, at an elevation of nine thousand

Environmentalists worry that jets in Lukla, Nepal are polluting sensitive Himalayan ecosystems.

Cholera: The Disease of the Ganges

For many decades, health professionals in India have attempted to prevent Hindus from bathing in or drinking the Ganges' water because it is highly polluted with human feces that can carry the deadly cholera bacterium *Vibrio cholerae*. Besides contracting the disease from contaminated water, humans who eat shellfish that have ingested particles of feces can also contract cholera. In 1950, cholera was one of the leading causes of death in India, killing 86,997 people. Today that number has declined because of medical intervention, but it remains a serious health risk.

Vibrio cholerae is particularly suited to the Ganges because it can survive for surprisingly long periods in contaminated water sources. It does not require an intermediary animal host or some form of agent for dispersal. Once ingested, it finds its way to human intestines where the bacteria produce a toxin that inhibits the absorption of water and salts. The bacteria then flush the intestines of water, causing severe dehydration. Without treatment, death can occur within hours.

feet. Used by thousands of trekkers and tourists, it is now the busiest mountain airfield in Nepal. Environmentalists object to the airstrip because the exhaust from the jets landing there is trapped in Himalayan valleys and pollutes the formerly clear air. This airstrip was partially built by Sir Edmund Hillary, the first man to climb Mount Everest, the world's tallest mountain. In an interview in 1999, Hillary was asked if he thought the airstrip had contributed to the commercialization of Mount Everest. Hillary admitted that this was probably the case, but argued that the overall effect had been positive:

> Our first airstrip was for a specific purpose. The United Nations wanted to fly in food for the hundreds of Tibetan refugees crossing over the border, but there was nowhere for aircraft to land. It is now the busiest mountain airfield in the whole of Nepal,

and thousands of trekkers and tourists fly in. I have sometimes wondered if establishing it has brought harm to the people of the Himalayas, but on the whole, when I think back, it has done quite a lot of good, too.[29]

To the ancient peoples of the Ganges Basin, who climbed up to the glaciers to pray and bathe in the sacred water, there was no greater crime than the desecration of the river. Despite all that is known today about the ravages of the river, the desecration continues. Fortunately, over the past twenty years, scientists and Indian policy makers have recognized the urgent need to reverse the damage.

5

....

Healing the Ganges

Caring for the Ganges so that it can serve future generations requires addressing the political, economic, and social needs of those who depend on the river without placing further strain on it in the future. To achieve these objectives, local and international agencies are now focusing on long-term solutions to the problems stemming from abuses that have degraded the river's waters.

The Ganges Action Plan

Hope for the Ganges rests with significantly reducing pollutants discharged into the river. This monumental task, which is recognized as essential by most of the scientific community, is now recognized as necessary by the Indian government as well. Together, the scientists and policy makers in India defined a series of steps called the Ganges Action Plan (GAP) to clean the river and bring life back to it.

In 1985, the GAP was launched by the late prime minister Rajiv Gandhi along with a commitment of $300 million. The plan highlighted the immediate need to build sewage treatment plants, electric crematoria, and public toilets in twenty major cities along the Ganges Basin that authorities identified as causing 90 percent of the pollution. The objective was to intercept, divert, and treat 220 million gallons of sewage per day, 66 percent of the total daily volume of sewage.

Water Treatment Facilities

In 1986, when Prime Minister Rajiv Gandhi allocated money to begin construction on the water treatment facilities, he highlighted the serious nature of the GAP:

> The Ganga is a symbol of our spirituality, our tradition, our tolerance and our synthesis. But it is the most polluted river with sewage and pollution from cities and industries thrown into it. From now, we shall put a stop to all this. We are launching the plan for the people of India.[30]

Engineers employed by the Indian government set out to clean the polluted water using a process called aerobic water treatment. This technology is a well-established approach to the elimination of organic pollutants by accelerating the decomposition of human wastes, dead plant and animal matter, and some forms of industrial contamination.

At the designated cities, large concrete tanks were constructed along the river at the point where the pollution discharged into the river was at its highest concentration. Each tank was capable of holding several million gallons of water. The process for cleaning the water first entailed pumping polluted water from the Ganges into the tanks. Once the water was in the tanks, a second set of pumps blasted air into the contaminated water through a system of aeration pipes. The heavy dose of air stimulated the growth of bacteria that decompose the highly toxic organic material into simpler substances that have a relatively low level of toxicity. When engineers testing the water determined that the bacteria had reduced the waters' toxicity to safe levels, the treated effluent was pumped back to the Ganges. The simplicity of the aerobic

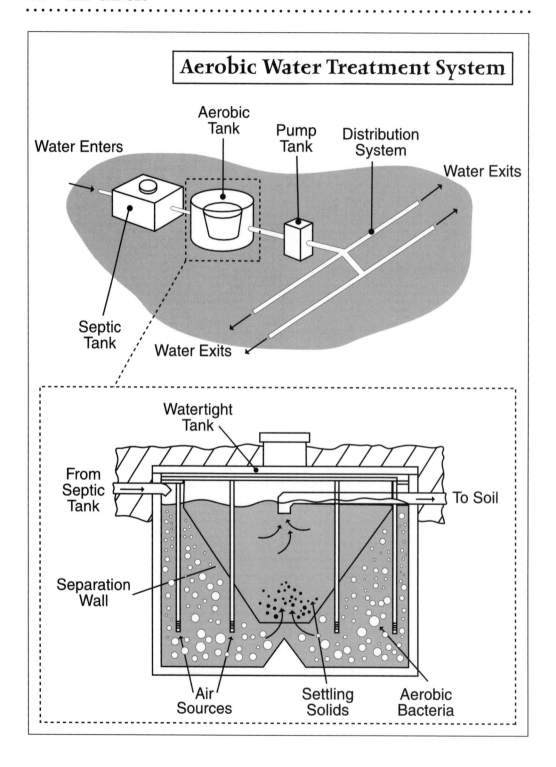

Aerobic Water Treatment System

Water Enters

Aerobic Tank

Pump Tank

Distribution System

Water Exits

Septic Tank

Water Exits

Watertight Tank

From Septic Tank

To Soil

Separation Wall

Air Sources

Settling Solids

Aerobic Bacteria

treatment of water was heralded as a success. Requiring little more than concrete tanks, electric pumps, and pipes, the water quality of the river improved.

Crematoria

The next element of the plan was the building of electric crematoria at the three major *tirthas*. One form of organic pollution that the GAP members hoped to reduce before it entered the Ganges was human corpses that had either been only partially cremated or not been burned at all. Members of the GAP knew that they could never ban the use of the Ganges for disposal of cremated remains because of the river's place in traditional Hindu beliefs. The best they could hope for was to eliminate the problem of partially cremated bodies in the river. In 1986, to promote complete cremation, the GAP members constructed electric pyres that would achieve complete cremation at far lower cost than traditional wood pyres. The cost for a complete wood cremation dropped from $100 to about $10 for an electric one. The idea was an immediate success as millions of poor Hindu families committed their dead family members to the electric heating elements. The river in turn experienced considerable relief from decomposing bodies.

Some Hindu priests, however, who consulted the twenty-five-hundred-year-old holy writings known as the *Veda*, believed that electric cremations were a sacrilege. The *Veda* specified cremation on wood pyres, not electric ones. After intense debate within the community of Hindu priests, the decision was reached that electric cremations would be considered in keeping with the proper spirit of cremation as described in the *Veda*.

Unfortunately for the Ganges River, some fundamental Hindus rejected the conclusion reached by the priests. Some partial wood cremations continued and burnt bodies remained part of the waterscape on the Ganges. Although their numbers were substantially reduced, something had to be done about them.

An illustration of a traditional wood pyre used to cremate bodies along the Ganges.

Eliminating Human Corpses

In 1988, two years after the introduction of electric crematoria, an estimated sixty thousand partially cremated corpses continued to float down the Ganges each year. To rid the river of them, GAP directors turned to zoologists for a solution. The zoologists studied the floating corpses and watched as circling vultures landed on them and picked at them as they traveled downriver. Hoping to find a solution less repugnant than vultures eating the bodies, biologists called in herpetologists and ichthyologists to study the problem.

Everyone involved hoped to find a species of carnivorous fish that could be introduced to the Ganges that would eat the corpses but not the bathers. Unfortunately, none of the known species, such as the piranha, could survive in the Ganges. Herpetologists, however, who studied the alligator snapping turtle, a 150-pound carnivore found in many waterways around the world, recommended it as the perfect scavenger to rid the Ganges of human bodies.

In 1989, herpetologists released thirty thousand alligator snapping turtles in a thirty-mile stretch of the Ganges downstream from Varanasi to consume the floating bodies. The turtles, which typically feed on fresh meat, had to become accustomed to eating decaying flesh. To train them, the turtles were first kept in a pond, where they were habituated to rotting fish before being released into the river. Herpetologists assured GAP officials that the reptiles would pose no danger to swimmers or bathers. Their predictions were correct; the snapping turtles were attracted to the rotting bodies and ate them but did not bother bathers.

Sweet Water Fish Farming

As steps were taken by the government to clean up the Ganges, entrepreneurs set to work rekindling the river's fishing industry. In the 1970s, when fishermen became aware that the depletion of fish stocks in the Ganges was due primarily to pollution, many developed pond fisheries far from the banks of the river. Growing fish in controlled clean water ponds is generally called aquaculture, but to the local fishermen managing the ponds, the industry is called sweet water fish farming. The name came from unpolluted water running off the Himalayas, known as sweet water to hydrologists. Many farmers living in the Delta own a sweet water pond in their backyards called a *pukura,* in which they raise fish for market.

The sweet water ponds are stocked with mature fish of one particular species per pond. Populating each pond with only one species of fish allows the farmer to tailor conditions in the pond to meet the needs of that one species and to eliminate the possibility of predation from other species. When the adults spawn and the young are hatched, they are isolated from their parents to avoid the common problem of adults eating the young. The young fish, called fry, are then fed a rich diet of food that promotes growth and keeps them healthy. Fed a nutritious diet, swimming in clean water, and safe from predators, the young mature more quickly than they would if they were in the river. Typically, young fish reach commercial size in about eight months, at which time the entire pond is drained through a system of nets that trap the fish. When the fish are sold, the ponds are refilled and the cycle begins again.

Estimates for 2001 indicate that 78 percent of inland fish production comes from sweet water fish farming. These farms have provided healthier fish than the fish caught in the Ganges and they provide a steady income stream to the farmers who raise them.

Rice Fish Farming

The newest form of fish farming to attract the attention of fishermen along the Ganges involves the integration of fish farming with the growing of rice. Agronomists have long noted that the flooded rice fields hold ample water for many small but commercially valuable fish to thrive alongside the shoots of rice plants. Scientists believe that combining the two food types can increase overall food production as well as increasing profits for the farmers.

Fish breeding in the flooded rice fields is not new. Rural people living in the Delta have fished for hundreds of years in and around flooded rice fields and have traditionally relied on this ready supply of protein during the wet season. The recent introduction of scientific rice fish farms, however, has created a much more efficient system that benefits both the rice and the fish.

Fish farms among the rice paddies involves setting up nylon nets around the perimeters of rice fields to contain fish and to prevent the entry of predators. As an alternative to enclosing entire fields with nets, some farmers prefer to place fish in large submerged cages. The water used for irrigation is often from the Ganges and is not as clean

as the water used in the sweet water farms, yet it does contain some of the natural foods eaten by the fish. To supplement the natural food, farmers sprinkle fish pellets over the water to fatten the fish. Before harvesting the rice, farmers move back and forth through the fields netting their scaly quarry.

A farmer raises a fish net from the water beside a rice field.

Integrating aquaculture and rice farming not only solved the problem of dwindling fish stocks, but also helped to alleviate hunger in India. Beginning in 1997, several Indian and international organizations agreed to team up to feed starving people in India. They initiated projects aimed at increasing and sustaining the productivity of rice and fish in the seasonally flooded ecosystem along the eastern Ganges, particularly in the Delta. The experiments involved 267 households, half of whom owned their own land while the other half were poor tenant farmers who rented the land. The average size of the fields was two and a half acres and the flood depths in the rice fields ranged from one to one-and-a-half feet. The average fish yield ranged from eight hundred to twelve hundred pounds per two-and-a-half-acre plot.

Enforcement of Pollution Laws

The authors of the GAP understood that money to clean the Ganges would be wasted unless the pollutants annually dumped into the river were significantly reduced. To achieve reasonable reductions, laws were passed imposing limits on types and daily volumes of chemicals that could be dumped into the river. Failure to comply with pollution laws was punishable by fines and in the case of gross violations, closure of the factory producing the pollution.

The industry against which politicians and environmentalists imposed the most severe restrictions was leather tanning. Activists singled out four factories along the 150-mile stretch from Barauni to the Farakka Barrage. These included the Bata shoe factory, which alone, in preparing leather for use in shoes, empties sixty-five thousand gallons of toxic chemical waste into the river each day. Factories were faced with the challenge of either using less-toxic chemicals in the tanning process or filtering wastewater to remove the toxins before returning it to the river.

The response to the new regulations was mixed. Eight years after the GAP imposed its restrictions on industries along the Ganges, some industries complied with pollution standards; others did not and were closed as a result. India's supreme court identified several industries located along the river that continued using the Ganges for dumping effluents on a large scale. The courts ruled against the industries and ordered the closure of 191 factories along the eastern Ganges and the closure of another 212 factories in and around the city of Agra. Leading Indian environmental activist and attorney Mahesh C. Mehta, who brought many lawsuits against polluters, stated in 1995 regarding the courts and the continuing problems of pollution:

It is a really big problem now. Many parts of the Ganges river are totally dead; the water is so polluted that it is unfit for drinking, washing, bathing or irrigational purposes. Thirty percent of the Ganges' pollution is being caused by industry. The Court has ordered the polluting factories to install pollution control devices, and many are now doing that. To a large extent, I have succeeded in seeing that industrial pollution is controlled.[31]

Hydroelectric Dams

India, along with all industrial nations, has developed an enormous appetite for electricity, but has never been able to generate enough to satisfy demand. Many generating plants that burn oil have been built throughout the country, including several along the Ganges. Tragically, oil seepage from these plants has found its way to the Ganges along with other toxins. One clean alternative to generating electricity by burning fossil fuels is hydroelectric dams.

India is a latecomer to hydroelectricity compared with many countries. Although a handful of small hydroelectric dams exists on the Ganges, collectively they fail to generate enough electricity to be considered major contributors to India's electrical supply. An example is the generators on the thirteen falls on Ganges Canal. These falls spread out along a two-hundred-mile stretch and have an average vertical drop of only nine feet to spin the generators that produce electricity. Although the volume of flow is significant, the short drops mean that the turbines collectively can only manage to generate a meager thirty-four megawatts of electricity.

In the 1990s, hoping to increase the supply of power and recognizing the importance of a long vertical drop to generate electricity, the Indian government entered negotiations with the government of Nepal to build a hydroelectric dam high up on the Mahakali River, a northern tributary of the Ganges emanating from the Himalayas.

Merging Modern Science with Ancient Religion

One of the biggest obstacles to the cleanup of the Ganges is convincing India's 800 million Hindus that the river is in need of help. Faithful Hindus consider the water sacred, and therefore, in no need of human assistance. For the past two decades, considerable frustration has been experienced by the scientific community in trying to impose scientific solutions on a spiritually minded community that believes no solutions are necessary.

A possible bridge spanning the gulf between science and religion is Veer Bhadra Mishra, who is both a Hindu priest and a scientist with a university degree in hydrology. Now living in India, he has made saving the Ganges his mission in life. His approach is unique because unlike most others, he has a keen under-standing of the religious significance of the river as well as the scientific significance of reversing the damage done by pollution.

In 1982 Mishra started the Swatch Ganga Campaign (SGC), and since then has almost single-handedly fought to adopt certain ways to clean the Ganges, especially downriver from the ghats in the larger cities where bathing and cremation are constant occurrences. Through the work of the SGC, Mishra has been able to gain international support for his cause. Of greater significance is that he has been one of the few men to receive the respect of both the scientific and religious communities.

In 1999, *Time* magazine named Mishra among the seven greatest heroes on the planet. The article

Named the Pancheshwar Dam, and begun in 1996, this one-thousand-foot-tall dam will generate 6,480 megawatts when it is completed in 2006. The agreement between the two countries calls for an equal division of the water, the electricity generated by the dam, and the estimated $12 billion cost.

East of the Pancheshwar Dam, a tributary of the Ganges called the Sapta Koshi (also Sapta Kosi) River, threads its way down the Himalayas until it joins the

Hindu worshippers gather along the Ganges River. Religious and scientific authorities agree that reforms are needed to help preserve the Ganges.

cited him as a man whose central passion for saving the Ganges unites his spirituality and his professional work. *Time* attributed his success to his position and experience as both the *Mahant*, the head of the Sankat Mochan Hindu temple, as well as the head of the engineering department at the Benares Hindu University.

Ganges at the city of Barah Kshetra. In 1981, a feasibility study financed by the Indian government recommended the construction at this site of a 3,275-foot-long concrete dam that will generate three thousand megawatts as its waters drop 875 feet to spin several large turbines. Construction is slated to start sometime before the completion of the Pancheshwar Dam.

The outlook for hydroelectricity is hopeful. However, what the engineers building the dams and environmentalists know all too well is that damming the river to generate electricity will simply further reduce flow downriver, contributing to problems with silt, pollution, and reduced navigability. Every change made to the river to accommodate India's rising population is done so at the expense of the river.

Epilogue
....

A Grim Forecast

The optimism that accompanied the start of the GAP in 1985 has largely faded away. The efforts toward improving the Ganges' water quality, producing healthier fish, and enforcing environmental laws have encountered more obstacles than were imagined by the GAP founders. Despite everyone's good intentions, the GAP has been plagued with problems, some of which could have been avoided and some of which could not have been.

The biggest problem that has arisen, which critics of GAP believe was avoidable, was the failure of engineers to calculate the amount of electricity needed to operate the heavy-duty pumps used at the many water treatment facilities. The large industrial pumps required to move water and to aerate it adequately consume far more electricity than can be supplied. The large water treatment facilities built at Hardwar, Varanasi, and Allahabad rarely function anymore due to electricity shortages. Additional power lines needed to run the pumps were never built. In any case, even when the electricity is available, the pumps often remain idle because many are clogged with plastic bags and plastic flowers used in cremation ceremonies.

Workers construct a hydroelectric dam in Sharavathi.

The same problem haunts the electric crematoria. Electrical failures have closed an estimated 90 percent of those built with GAP money, and bodies continue to float down the Ganges in large numbers.

Smaller yet equally frustrating problems have also plagued the GAP. In the city of Patna, for example, the public toilets built with GAP money have been converted into offices, and the ponds built to treat polluted water have been drained and now serve as sports fields. Of even greater frustration to GAP members, the thirty thousand alligator snapping turtles that initially fed on corpses have all disappeared into the soup pots of poachers.

Few independent scientists who have studied the current condition of the Ganges express optimism for the river. A recent study investigating the GAP debacle found that the amount of sewage flowing into the Ganges has doubled since 1985. The same study found evidence of widespread corruption among government officials who are siphoning off funds earmarked for the project. Attorney and environmental activist M.C. Mehta believes that the politicians have failed the people they are supposed to serve: "The people are helpless; the institutions have failed.... There is no political will to clean up the environment. Politicians are close to industrialists and their parties are funded by industrialists. They put pressure on the official agencies to adopt a soft attitude towards the polluting industries."[32]

Demographers predict that the quality of the Ganges will continue to decline rather than improve. They point out that the population of the Ganges Basin, which stood at 400 million in the year 2000, will be 1 billion in 2050. The river will be even more stressed in the future than it was in the past. According to a report in the *Economic Times*, an Indian newspaper, industrial discharge into the Ganges is growing at the rate of 8 percent per year. At this rate, by 2030, 1 billion gallons of untreated human and industrial effluents will enter the river every day.

Anil Kumar Tiwari, an environmental scientist at Allahabad University, stated in 2001, "The authorities claim that almost all industrial units are diverting their effluent to treatment plants ... but the ground reality is that their claim is exaggerated."[33] And according to science writer John Chalmers,

> According to a recent official government report, ... [GAP] has met only 39 percent of its primary target for sewage treatment. It said that less than half of the grossly polluting industrial units lining the 1,560-mile river had installed effluent treatment plants, and over 18 percent of them did not function properly.[34]

As the twenty-first century dawns, no new solutions to the problems of the Ganges are available, while the population continues to place greater demands on the river than ever before. Unlike several other major rivers of the world experiencing the ravages of pollution, the plight of the Ganges has not yet attracted the international attention given to the Nile, Amazon, and Yangtze. Until the world community perceives the need to protect the Ganges, it is unlikely that any improvements will be made by those dependent on *Ma Ganga*.

Notes

········

Introduction: Troubled Sacred Water

1. The Water Page, "River Ganges." www.thewaterpage.com.

Chapter 1: The River from Ice

2. Quoted in Stephen Darian, *The Ganges in Myth and History.* Honolulu: The University Press of Hawaii, 1978, p. 109.

Chapter 2: The Waters of Creation

3. Herodotus, *The Persian Wars,* Trans. George Rawlinson. New York: Modern Library, 1942, book 3, para. 106.
4. Herodotus, *The Persian Wars,* Trans. George Rawlinson. New York: Modern Library, 1942, book 7, para. 65.
5. Strabo, *Geography*, trans. Horace Jones. Cambridge, MA: Harvard University Press, 1967, book 15, para. 37.
6. Gregory L. Possehl, "Life in One of India's First Urban Societies," *Pennsylvania Gazette*, February 1997, p. 23.
7. Quoted in Darian, *The Ganges in Myth and History*, p. 90.
8. Quoted in Darian, *The Ganges in Myth and History*, p. 96.
9. Quoted in Darian, *The Ganges in Myth and History*, p. 14.
10. Quoted in Darian, *The Ganges in Myth and History*, p. 14.
11. Quoted in Darian, *The Ganges in Myth and History*, p. 13.
12. Quoted in Darian, *The Ganges in Myth and History*, p. 11.
13. Quoted in Darian, *The Ganges in Myth and History*, p. 109.

Chapter 3: Harnessing the Ganges

14. Cool Planet, "The Clothes Line." www.oxfam.org.
15. Quoted in H.W. Dickinson, "United States Patents the Steamboat, Monopoly and Litigation to Which It Gave Rise, Steamboat Enterprise in Europe and Asia," December 1996. www.history.rochester.edu.

16. Henry T. Bernstein, *Steamboats on the Ganges: An Exploration of the History of India's Modernization Through Science and Technology.* Calcutta: Orient Longman, 1987, p. 231.
17. Quoted in Bret Wallach, *Losing Asia: Modernization and the Culture of Development.* Baltimore: Johns Hopkins University Press, 1996, p. 83.
18. Quoted in Wallach, *Losing Asia,* p. 86.

Chapter 4: A River in Distress

19. *Time,* "The Bite of the Turtle," October 12, 1987, p. 46.
20. Quoted in Priya Raja, "The Ganga Clean-Up Act," 2002. www.nationalgeographic.com.
21. Advisory Council on the Environment, Water Policy and Planning Group Environmental Protection Department, "Opening Up ACE Meetings to the Public," July 2000. www.info.gov.
22. Ganges Forum Schedule, "India's holiest body of water is dangerously polluted. Will we be able to cleanse the sacred river?" November 1998. http://members.tripod.com.
23. Sankat Mochan Foundation, "Ganga Pollution." http://members.tripod.com.
24. Quoted in S.S. Jeevan, "Orphans of the River," *Down to Earth,* Feburary 15, 2002, p. 31.
25. Jeevan, "Orphans of the River," p. 30.
26. Jeevan, "Orphans of the River," p. 29.
27. Jeevan, "Orphans of the River," p. 29.
28. Quoted in Environmental News Network, "Bengal Tigers Face Shrinking Refuge, Food Supply," October 16, 2000. www.cnn.com.
29. Quoted in Allison Chase and Gordon Brown, "The Man Who Knocked the Bastard Off," *Outside,* October 1999, p. 28.

Chapter 5: Healing the Ganges

30. Quoted in Darryl D'Monte, "Filthy Flows the Ganga," *People & the Planet,* January 1996, p. 28.

31. M.C. Mehta, "Harnessing the Law To Clean Up India," *International Monitor,* July/August 1995, p. 87.

Epilogue: A Grim Forecast
32. Quoted in D'Monte, "Filthy Flows the Ganga," p. 28.
33. Quoted in John Chalmers, "India's Ganges: A Holy River of Pollution," January 13, 2001. www.cnn.com.
34. Chalmers, "India's Ganges: A Holy River of Pollution."

For Further Reading

Henry T. Bernstein, *Steamboats on the Ganges: An Exploration of the History of India's Modernization Through Science and Technology.* Calcutta: Orient Longman, 1987. Bernstein's book traces all present technological and industrial advances in India back to the arrival of the British during the European industrial revolution. Bernstein believes that the arrival of the British steamboats began India's march toward factories and industry that play a role both in India's economic development as well as in the massive pollution of the Ganges.

Gina Douglas, *The Ganges.* Sussex, England: Scott Foresman, 1978. The author has provided a basic work on the geography of the Ganges, its animals, how the river is of importance to the Indians, and its force in the spiritual lives of all Hindus. The book includes good maps and a selection of color photographs.

Jay S. Fine, *Monsoons.* New York: John Wiley, 1987. The author provides a detailed yet readable account of all climatic conditions causing monsoons around the world as well as discussions about their impact on agriculture and the lives of people living in monsoon regions.

Raghubir Singh, *The Ganges.* New York: Aperture, 1992. This book is primarily a photo essay of the Ganges and its peoples. The photographs are of the highest professional quality, and interspersed with the many colorful photographs is text that provides a good narrative of the river and its importance in the lives of Indians.

Works Consulted

Books

Stephen Darian, *The Ganges in Myth and History*. Honolulu: The University Press of Hawaii, 1978. This is an excellent book that addresses the history, hydrology, pollution, and spiritual significance of the Ganges.

Herodotus, *The Persian Wars*. Trans. George Rawlinson. New York: Modern Library, 1942. The first half of this famous work describes Herodotus's travels throughout Egypt, India, and Mesopotamia while the second half focuses on the Persian invasion of Greece during the early fifth century B.C.

Edmund Hillary, *From the Ocean to the Sky*. New York: Viking Press, 1979. This work, written by the first man to climb Mount Everest, is a-true life adventure story documenting his boat trip from the mouth of the Ganges to its source. Hillary describes the physical characteristics of the river as well as the people living along the river's banks.

A. Markandya and M.N. Murty, *Cleaning Up the Ganges: A Cost Benefit Analysis of the Ganga Action Plan*. Delhi, India: Oxford University Press, 2000. This book represents the analyses and thoughts of many experts in water engineering, fisheries, biodiversity, health, and economics. It is a sophisticated academic work encompassing all disciplines that relate to the Ganges: environmental economics, policy making, sociology, chemistry, and biology.

John Robert McNeill, *Something New Under the Sun: An Environmental History of the Twentieth-Century World*. New York: W.W. Norton, 2000. Professor McNeill's book is an excellent work documenting the causes of the world's pollution for the past one hundred years. He attributes nearly all of it to the industrialized and developing nations of the world. In this book, he has much to say about the plight of the Ganges.

Strabo, *Geography*. Trans. Horace Jones. Cambridge, MA: Harvard University Press, 1967. This is one of the great early books on geography recording Strabo's journeys throughout the known world. Strabo makes many fascinating observations about foreign lands, wildlife, geography, and the native populations.

Bret Wallach, *Losing Asia: Modernization and the Culture of Development*. Baltimore: Johns Hopkins University Press, 1996. Professor Wallach combines his geography and anthropology backgrounds as he travels through India observing canals, dams, mountains, rivers, farms, and peoples' ways of life. This is an excellent book for understanding why the people of India live as they do.

Periodicals

Allison Chase and Gordon Brown, "The Man Who Knocked the Bastard Off," *Outside*, October 1999.

Darryl D'Monte, "Filthy Flows the Ganga," *People & the Planet*, January 1996.

Joel T. Harper, Neil F. Humphrey, and W. Tad Pfeffer, "Three-Dimensional Deformation Measured in an Alaskan Glacier," *Science*, August 28, 1998.

Daniel R. Headrick, "The Tools of Imperialism: Technology and the Expansion of European Colonial Empires in the Nineteenth Century," *Journal of Modern History*, June 1979.

S.S. Jeevan, "Orphans of the River," *Down to Earth*, February 15, 2002.

M.C. Mehta, "Harnessing the Law to Clean Up India," *International Monitor*, July/August 1995.

Gregory L. Possehl, "Life in One of India's First Urban Societies," *Pennsylvania Gazette*, February 1997.

Time, "The Bite of the Turtle," October 12, 1987.

Websites

Advisory Council on the Environment (www.info.gov). This website references and provides a large selection of scientific papers that are delivered throughout the world on environmental studies and pressing environmental concerns.

CNN.com (www.cnn.com). This is the website of the CNN news agency. It provides current news from around the world reporting on significant events including politics, economics, religion, the environment, travel, and technology.

Cool Planet (www.oxfam.org). This educational website provides well-documented stories about unusual and interesting events around the world focusing on human rights, the environment, and new technology. The site also provides an array of maps, posters, poetry, and other educational tools.

Earth Crash Earth Spirit (http://eces.org). This website provides environmental links featuring articles on endangered areas of the world, books, photographs, and lectures.

Environmental News Network (www.enn.com). Environmental News Network (ENN) works to educate the world about environmental issues facing the planet. The ENN site offers timely environmental news, live chats, interactive quizzes, daily feature stories, forums for debate, and audio and video productions. The site is primarily an educational site.

Ganges Forum Schedule (http://members.tripod.com). This website was established to bring attention to a seminar held at the Illinois Institute of Technology in Chicago called, "The River Ganges and the Pollution Problem." The date of the seminar was November 7, 1998.

International Rivers Network (www.irn.org). The International Rivers Network supports local communities working to protect their rivers and watersheds. The website provides current information on what it views to be destructive river development projects, and it encourages alternate methods of meeting needs for water, energy, and flood management.

National Geographic (www.nationalgeographic.com). The National Geographic website provides similar stories as appear in the magazine of the same name. All stories feature nature around the world. Stories typically highlight animals, phenomena of the earth, medicine, and the lives of unusual peoples.

Sankat Mochan Foundation (http://members.tripod.com). The Sankat Mochan Foundation is a nonprofit organization founded in 1982 at Varanasi, India. It has been working to alleviate the environmental degradation of the Ganges. The foundation's objective is to restore the Ganges to its pristine purity that it enjoyed prior to the industrial revolution.

The Water Page (www.thewaterpage.com). The Water Page is an independent website dedicated to the promotion of sustainable water resources management and use. Its primary focus is on the rivers of Africa and other developing nations.

The Week (www.the-week.com). This website is an electronic version of the weekly Indian magazine, *The Week*. It provides articles covering current developments in Indian politics, economy, and culture.

Index

· · · · · · · ·

Picture Credits

• • • • • • • • • • • • • • • • • • •

About the Author

James Barter is the author of more than a dozen nonfiction books for middle school students. He received his undergraduate degree in history and classics at the University of California Berkeley, followed by graduate studies in ancient history and archaeology at the University of Pennsylvania. Mr. Barter has taught history as well as Latin and Greek.

A Fulbright scholar at the American Academy in Rome, Mr. Barter worked on archaeological sites in and around the city as well as on sites in the Naples area. Mr. Barter also has worked and traveled extensively in Greece.

Mr. Barter currently lives in Rancho Santa Fe, California, with his seventeen-year-old daughter, Kalista.